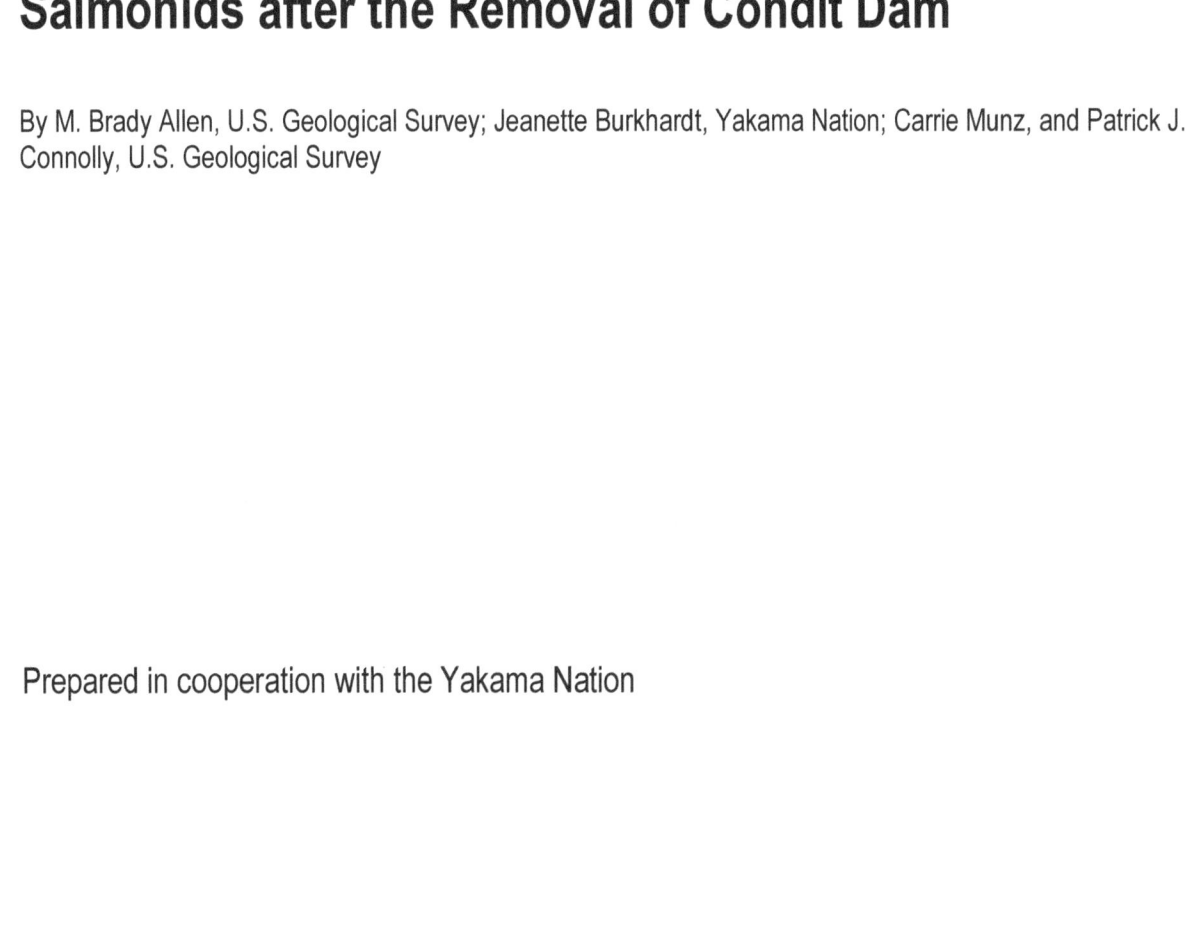

Fish Population and Habitat Analysis in Buck Creek, Washington, Prior to Recolonization by Anadromous Salmonids after the Removal of Condit Dam

By M. Brady Allen, U.S. Geological Survey; Jeanette Burkhardt, Yakama Nation; Carrie Munz, and Patrick J. Connolly, U.S. Geological Survey

Prepared in cooperation with the Yakama Nation

Open-File Report 2012–1270

U.S. Department of the Interior
U.S. Geological Survey

U.S. Department of the Interior
KEN SALAZAR, Secretary

U.S. Geological Survey
Marcia K. McNutt, Director

U.S. Geological Survey, Reston, Virginia: 2012

For more information on the USGS—the Federal source for science about the Earth,
its natural and living resources, natural hazards, and the environment—visit
http://www.usgs.gov or call 1–888–ASK–USGS

For an overview of USGS information products, including maps, imagery, and publications,
visit http://www.usgs.gov/pubprod

To order this and other USGS information products, visit http://store.usgs.gov

Contents

Figures

Tables

Conversion Factors and Datums

Conversion Factors

Inch/Pound to SI

Multiply	By	To obtain
Length		
foot (ft)	0.3048	meter (m)
Flow rate		
cubic foot per second (ft^3/s)	0.02832	cubic meter per second (m^3/s)

SI to Inch/Pound

Multiply	By	To obtain
Length		
centimeter (cm)	0.3937	inch (in.)
millimeter (mm)	0.03937	inch (in.)
meter (m)	3.281	foot (ft)
meter (m)	1.094	yard (yd)
kilometer (km)	0.6214	mile (mi)
kilometer (km)	0.5400	mile, nautical (nmi)
Area		
square meter (m^2)	0.0002471	acre
square meter (m^2)	10.76	square foot (ft^2)
square kilometer (km^2)	247.1	acre
square kilometer (km^2)	0.3861	square mile (mi^2)
Mass		
gram (g)	0.03527	ounce, avoirdupois (oz)

Temperature in degrees Celsius (°C) may be converted to degrees Fahrenheit (°F) as follows:
°F=(1.8×°C)+32

Datums

Vertical coordinate information is referenced to the World Geodetic System of 1984 (WGS84) datum.
Horizontal coordinate information is referenced to the WGS84 EGM96 geoid.
Altitude, as used in this report, refers to distance above the vertical datum.
Concentrations of chemical constituents in water are given either in milligrams per liter (mg/L) or micrograms per liter (µg/L).

Fish Population and Habitat Analysis in Buck Creek, Washington, Prior to Recolonization by Anadromous Salmonids after the Removal of Condit Dam

By M. Brady Allen, U.S. Geological Survey; Jeanette Burkhardt, Yakama Nation; Carrie Munz, and Patrick J. Connolly, U.S. Geological Survey

Abstract

We assessed the physical and biotic conditions in the part of Buck Creek, Washington, potentially accessible to anadromous fishes. This creek is a major tributary to the White Salmon River upstream of Condit Dam, which was breached in October 2011. Habitat and fish populations were characterized in four stream reaches. Reach breaks were based on stream gradient, water withdrawals, and fish barriers. Buck Creek generally was confined, with a single straight channel and low sinuosity. Boulders and cobble were the dominant stream substrate, with limited gravel available for spawning. Large-cobble riffles were 83 percent of the available fish habitat. Pools, comprising 15 percent of the surface area, mostly were formed by bedrock with little instream cover and low complexity. Instream wood averaged 6—10 pieces per 100 meters, 80 percent of which was less than 50 centimeters in diameter. Water temperature in Buck Creek rarely exceeded 16 degrees Celsius and did so for only 1 day at river kilometer (rkm) 3 and 11 days at rkm 0.2 in late July and early August 2009. The maximum temperature recorded was 17.2 degrees Celsius at rkm 0.2 on August 2, 2009. Minimum summer discharge in Buck Creek was 3.3 cubic feet per second downstream of an irrigation diversion (rkm 3.1) and 7.7 cubic feet per second at its confluence with the White Salmon River. Rainbow trout (*Oncorhynchus mykiss*) was the dominant fish species in all reaches. The abundance of age-1 or older rainbow trout was similar between reaches. However, in 2009 and 2010, the greatest abundance of age-0 rainbow trout (8 fish per meter) was in the most downstream reach. These analyses in Buck Creek are important for understanding the factors that may limit fish abundance and productivity, and they will help identify and prioritize potential restoration actions. The data collected constitute baseline information of pre-dam removal conditions that will allow assessment of changes in fish populations now that Condit Dam has been removed and anadromous fish have an opportunity to recolonize Buck Creek.

Introduction

The October 2011 breach of Condit Dam on the White Salmon River removed a significant fish passage barrier at river kilometer (rkm) 5.3 of the basin allowing fish passage for the first time in nearly a century (fig. 1). The reopening of fish passage affords an opportunity to regain an important drainage basin for Endangered Species Act (ESA)-listed ("Threatened") salmon stocks: lower Columbia Chinook (*Oncorhynchus tshawytscha*) and coho salmon (*O. kisutch*), Columbia River chum salmon (*O. keta*), and middle Columbia River steelhead (*O. mykiss*) (National Marine Fisheries Service, 2005).

Buck Creek, one of the largest tributaries of the White Salmon River in the historical range of anadromous salmonids, is a tributary that enters the river from the west at rkm 7.5, near the upstream end of (former) Northwestern Lake, the reservoir that was formed by Condit Dam. Buck Creek was the only significant tributary with anadromous potential for which an assessment had not been completed when this study began. An assessment was completed in Rattlesnake Creek, the other main tributary with anadromous potential (Allen and others, 2006). Normandeau and Associates (2004) reported that Buck Creek had substantial historical potential for steelhead, Chinook salmon, and coho salmon. Upland and riparian habitat data for Buck Creek have been collected sporadically by various entities including Washington Department of Natural Resources (DNR) and the Underwood Conservation District. However, published information on fish population, and riparian and instream habitat was unavailable. Therefore, the Yakama Nation funded collaborative efforts with the U.S. Geological Survey (USGS) to conduct an assessment of existing fish habitat and resident fish populations in Buck Creek for potential recolonization by anadromous fish. This baseline survey of resident fish populations and the habitat that supports them was considered an important first step in assessing how conducive conditions might be to support anadromous fish. The assessment of fish populations before and after dam removal could aid in understanding steelhead and resident trout population dynamics as well as the contribution of resident trout to ESA-listed steelhead populations in Buck Creek.

Steelhead habitat needs vary by life stage, and the habitat conditions necessary to support each life stage must be present or accessible for a population to be viable. If any one of these habitat conditions is reduced enough to cause density-dependent mortality for any part of the life history, then this bottleneck, as conceived by Hall and Baker (1982), will prevent the fish population from reaching its potential abundance. The habitat condition that reduces abundance would be considered a limiting factor to reaching the potential abundance. The life history of steelhead trout can be separated into several life stages that have distinct habitat needs. Juvenile *O. mykiss* can either migrate to the sea as steelhead (anadromy) or can remain in freshwater as rainbow trout. In Washington, those *O. mykiss* that are anadromous usually spend 1–3 years in freshwater, with the greatest proportion spending 2 years in freshwater (Busby and others, 1996). Because of this life history and their year-round presence in streams, steelhead greatly depend on the quality and quantity of freshwater habitat. Many of the early steelhead life-stage habitat requirements are identical to those of resident rainbow trout (Raleigh and others, 1984). Therefore, the limiting factors for rainbow trout for the first few years of rearing in Buck Creek should be similar to those of recolonizing steelhead. Resident rainbow trout potentially could even contribute to the brood stock for recolonizing steelhead.

Despite apparent associations between habitat condition and the status of fish populations, it has been difficult for researchers explicitly to link abundance or population health with habitat characteristics. In other studies, the perception of which habitat traits were important was a function of the scale of observation (Feist and others, 2003). Factors other than physical habitat characteristics—such as nutrients, food availability, water chemistry, and predation—also may limit fish abundance. Even when the habitat requirements of individual life stages are well-defined, the population-level consequences of habitat change are uncertain because only a subset of habitats usually will limit a population at any given time (Rosenfeld, 2003). Therefore, identification of a specific habitat condition as a primary limiting factor can be problematic, particularly without information about the historical stream conditions. Because of these uncertainties, we believe that the habitat conditions that are typical of the streams draining unmanaged forests are the standard by which to set target conditions. These conditions also could be considered "properly functioning conditions" (PFC). Recognizing that returning a degraded drainage basin to an unmanaged or pristine state would be unlikely, the PFC concept, created originally by the Bureau of Land Management, is intended to be a guideline for restoring the natural habitat-forming processes to riparian and wetland areas (Prichard and others, 1993). This approach does not seek to optimize the stream environment for a particular species or age class, but assumes that naturally functioning and ecologically intact channels will provide long-term sustainability for diverse fish assemblages (Peterson and others, 1992; Williams and others, 1997; Beechie and Bolton, 1999).

The Ecosystem Diagnosis and Treatment (EDT) model (Mobrand, 2002) was used in the White Salmon River to predict salmon and steelhead productivity and abundance after Condit Dam was removed (Allen and Connolly, 2005). The EDT model allows the user to rate the quality, quantity, and diversity of fish habitat within reaches of a stream by rating 46 environmental attributes for historical and current conditions. Many information sources were used to rate the 46 attributes in the White Salmon River (Allen and Connolly, 2005). Much of the information used for the EDT model in Buck Creek, last run on April 12, 2004, was a result of a review of existing references and a brief field habitat survey conducted by USGS and Washington Department of Fish and Wildlife (Allen and Connolly, 2005). The model was used to help prioritize reaches for restoration and to identify data gaps. The results of the model also were used to describe habitat conditions for salmon and steelhead in the White Salmon River Subbasin Plan (Normandeau and Associates, 2004). Because the information used in the EDT model for Buck Creek was sparse, we collected habitat information in Buck Creek in this study that can further refine the model inputs for that assessment.

The goal of this study was to assess salmonid (primarily *O. mykiss*) population size and health and to assess instream and riparian habitat conditions prior to recolonization by anadromous salmonids. More specifically, the objectives of this study were to: (1) gain information about abundance, productivity, life histories, diseases, and genetic composition of the existing juvenile salmonid populations, concentrating primarily, but not exclusively, on *O. mykiss* in reaches of the potentially anadromous portion of Buck Creek; (2) characterize stream and riparian habitat conditions in Buck Creek that will be accessible to anadromous salmonids; and (3) refine the information used in the EDT model to assist in prioritizing future restoration activities.

Description of Study Site

Buck Creek, a tributary to the White Salmon River in south-central Washington State, flows into the White Salmon River from the west at rkm 7.5 (fig. 1), upstream of former Northwestern Lake, which was the reservoir impounded behind Condit Dam. The Buck Creek drainage basin is in steep, mountainous terrain forming the foothills of the Cascade Range just south of Mount Adams. The total area of the drainage basin is 36 km^2, about 90 percent of which has been managed by Washington Department of Natural Resources since 1921. Altitude within the drainage basin ranges from 92 m at its mouth to 610 m at the upper end of the potential anadromous zone (near the city of White Salmon's concrete water diversion dam at rkm 6.4), and 1,219 m at its headwaters. Annual precipitation throughout the drainage basin averages 152 cm. The gradient of most slopes in the drainage basin ranges from 30 to 90 percent. Buck Creek is in the transitional ecotone between the moderate coastal maritime climate zone and the continental inland climate zone (Normandeau and Associates, 2004). The drainage basin has second-growth, mixed conifer and deciduous forests and steep canyons with incised basalt bedrock channels. There are few areas where the creek may access anything that could be described as a floodplain. The drainage basin has a high road density relative to many basins (3.2 km/km^2), with 49 km of unpaved access roads, most which were used by DNR for timber hauling and forest management activities (Allen and Connolly, 2005, appendix A). Additionally, there are 18.3 km of mostly unregulated recreational trails. Since 1923, the city of White Salmon has been diverting water for its municipal supply from Buck Creek, with a 10-year hiatus during 2000—2010 owing to surface-water contamination. Buck Creek was used again as the supply source for water consumption on July 23, 2010, after the Buck Creek sand filtration plant was completed, at an altitude of 327 m, downstream of the city's concrete headworks dam.

We divided Buck Creek into four reaches based on geomorphology and man-made or natural fish barriers (fig. 1; table 1). The gradient and valley confinement is lowest in Reach 1, which begins at the confluence with the White Salmon River and extends upstream 0.9 km to a change in valley confinement. However, we did not have permission to sample the properties from the end of Reach 1, at rkm 0.2, to the DNR property boundary, at rkm 2.0. Reach 2 was confined by valley walls and extended from rkm 2.0 to rkm 3.1, where there was a 1.1-m high irrigation diversion (0.76-m-high concrete dam with 0.35-m-high wooden flash boards). This irrigation diversion has a 4.5-ft^3/s water right (Aspect Consulting, 2011). Reach 3 extends from rkm 3.1 to a 4.3-m-high waterfall at rkm 5.0. There is a 1.3-m-high waterfall 27 m downstream of the larger waterfall (Plummer and Zuckerman, 2011). Reach 4 extends from rkm 5.0 to a 6-m-high waterfall at rkm 6.4 (the likely end of anadromy), a few meters downstream of the city of White Salmon municipal water facility.

Study Methods

Habitat Surveys

To conduct stream habitat and wood surveys, we walked the stream channel and measured a series of variables at 20-m intervals and 100-m intervals. At each 20-m interval, we measured stream width and visually estimated canopy shading over the entire 20-m section from the stream center. When estimating the percent shade, we also estimated the percent resulting from conifer or hardwood vegetation. Within each 20-m interval, we measured stream gradient, the length of each habitat type, and the mean and maximum stream depth of each habitat unit. Definitions for declaring stream habitat types (riffles, glides, and pools) generally followed methods of Washington State's Timber, Fish, and Wildlife Monitoring Program Method Manual (TFW) Habitat Unit survey (Bisson and others, 1982; Pleus and others, 1999; Lestelle and others, 2004). Fast-water habitat types were defined as glides, large-cobble riffle (dominant substrate larger than 12 cm in diameter), or small-cobble riffle (dominant substrate smaller than 12 cm in diameter). Slow-water habitat types were defined as pools. Less common habitat types included in the survey were beaver ponds, alcoves, off-channel habitats such as side channels, oxbows, and backwater pools. In each habitat unit, we measured the wetted width, mean depth, and maximum depth. Additionally, in pools, we quantified the pool tailout depth and the percent of the wetted channel surface area comprising the pool tailout, and estimated the percentage of instream and overhead fish cover. The amount of instream fish cover in pools was further defined by the percentage contributed by large wood (>30 cm in diameter), small wood (<30 cm in diameter), substrate, undercut bank, or other. Within each 20-m interval, we noted indications of hydromodification (such as road fill, bridge abutments, or other man-made structures within or adjacent to the stream channel), water withdrawals, and altered riparian function as defined in Lestelle and others (2004). A second, more experienced crew randomly surveyed several sections in each reach to ensure the accuracy of the visually estimated habitat variables.

We characterized stream substrate, riparian vegetation, and channel confinement at 10-m transects every 100 m in Reaches 2, 3, and 4. Because the total length of Reach 1 that we had permission to survey was less than 200 m, transects in this reach were characterized at 20-m intervals. We documented the dominant and subdominant species of riparian vegetation within the adjacent riparian zone (a cross-channel transect 0–3 m from bankfull width by 10 m wide) and the outer riparian zone (a transect 3–10 m from bankfull width by 10 m wide). Channel confinement was measured as the distance from the wetted width to the bankfull width, to terraces, and to hillslopes. The height from the water surface to the bankfull width and the first terrace were measured. Substrate composition was evaluated using the transect method of the salmonid spawning habitat availability survey protocol (Schuett-Hames and others, 1999a).

A large woody debris (LWD) survey was conducted in conjunction with the stream and habitat surveys by physically measuring each downed piece of wood larger than 10 cm in diameter and 2 m in length within the bankfull width. We generally followed the methods in TFW's Large Woody Debris Survey (Schuett-Hames and others, 1999c). As with the habitat survey, the LWD survey was collected in high resolution (the dataset contains the size, location, type, stability, and function of each qualifying piece), which was intended to help managers with site-specific restoration and as a reference to assess the degree of change in future conditions. A summary of the LWD survey is provided in this document.

We attempted to collect McNeil core samples to assess the quality of spawning substrate at the sites previously identified during habitat surveys as containing suitable spawning substrate. We were unable to sink the sampler to the minimum depth necessary for operation because of the large underlying substrate at the eight sites where core samples were attempted. Because we were unable to collect McNeil core samples for analysis using TFW Salmonid Spawning Gravel Composition Survey methodology (Schuett-Hames and others, 1999b), results were not included in this report.

In the Pacific Northwest, a regionally calibrated 10-metric index of biological integrity has been developed based on benthic invertebrates (benthic index of biological integrity or B-IBI; Kleindl, 1995; Fore and others, 1996; Karr, 1998). Macroinvertebrate samples were collected in each reach of the Buck Creek drainage at the locations listed in table 1. All samples were collected using a 500-µm mesh Surber net with a one-square-foot base. Samples were then stored in 80 percent ethanol. Ecoanalysts, Inc. (Moscow, Idaho) identified all macroinvertebrate species and evaluated each sample using the B-IBI method, which was developed to show health of a water body based on the macroinvertebrate assemblages found in the basin (Karr and others, 1986; Morley, 2000). The B-IBI scoring system is a quantitative method for comparing the water quality and overall stream health based on the biological condition of streams (Karr and others, 1986). This method uses a series of metrics, such as the number of long-lived taxa, to establish a single integrated score that quantifies overall water quality. For calculating the B-IBI, the Species-Genus procedure was used (Puget Sound Stream Benthos, 2012a), along with the attributes from Puget Sound Benthos (2012b). Because the B-IBI is a standardized scoring system, it can be used to compare and rank the health of different streams or stream reaches.

Stream temperatures were collected hourly by Onset HOBO® automated temperature recording devices, which were deployed in Reach 1 (rkm 0.2) by the Underwood Conservation District and in Reach 2 (rkm 2.9), Reach 3 (rkm 3.3), and Reach 4 (rkm 5.4) by the Yakama Nation Timber, Fish, and Wildlife Program (table 1). In Reach 4, the temperature recording device was lost and the data were not available.

Stream discharge measurements were taken within the same day in each reach every 2 weeks during the low-flow period in 2008 and 2009 (table 1). These data were used to characterize temporal and spatial patterns of flow during late spring through early autumn (June–October) along the stream continuum. Stream discharge measurements were taken at the Big Buck Creek Road bridge (Reach 1, rkm 0.2), 50 m downstream of the irrigation diversion (Reach 2, rkm 2.9), 20 m upstream of the first bridge on Buck Creek Road (Reach 3, rkm 3.3), and 20 m upstream of the Buck Creek trailhead footbridge (Reach 4, rkm 5.4). Following the protocol of Bain and Stevenson (1999), we anchored a measuring tape perpendicular to streamflow and recorded the distance to the left and right wetted edge. We measured water depth and velocity with a Marsh-McBirney® Flo-Mate model 2000 flow meter at a minimum of 15 intervals (although usually at about 20 intervals) along the measuring tape to insure that no more than 7 percent of flow was represented in any one cell. Because water depths never exceeded 1 m, water velocities were measured at 60 percent of the depth at each interval as described by Bain and Stevenson (1999).

To estimate discharge at our streamflow monitoring stations, flow was computed by summing the flows of intervals, where the flow at each interval was calculated using the equation:

$$Q_n = d_n \times \left(\frac{b_{n+1} - b_{n-1}}{2} \right) \times v_n ,$$

(1)

Where

Q_n = discharge at interval n,

d_n = water depth at interval n,

b_n = distance along the tape measure from the left wetted edge to point n, and

v_n = mean velocity in interval n.

Fish Surveys

We estimated population abundance and biomass of resident salmonids for each of the four study reaches in Buck Creek in 2009 and 2010. We estimated population abundance and biomass of fish using the mark-recapture method as detailed in Temple and Pearsons (2007). We anchored two block nets, with each spanning the creek, about 2 m apart at the downstream end of each section. The upstream net was made of 7-mm knotless nylon mesh, and the downstream net was made of 3-mm nylon mesh. The lead line of each net was secured to the stream bottom with cobble and boulders, and fence posts or rebar were used to stabilize and support each net at least 0.5 m above the water surface. Another two nets were placed in a similar manner about 200 m upstream of the downstream end nets to ensure no fish immigration or emigration (that is, to ensure a closed population) during the estimation process. On most occasions, the entire section was electrofished and fish were marked in 1 day, the block nets were cleaned and left overnight, and the section was re-electrofished to recapture fish the following day. This process allowed for a minimum recovery period of 18 hours. In 2009, Reach 2 was an exception, because we were not able to complete the entire section in one day. We returned to the section the following morning to complete the first upstream pass, let the section recover overnight, and conducted our recapture pass the following day.

Each reach was electrofished in one slow, methodical upstream pass using a battery-powered Smith-Root® model 12-B backpack electrofisher. The electrofisher settings were 60 hertz, 6 milliseconds, and 300 volts. Two to three crew members with dip nets remained downstream of the electrofisher and netted stunned fish. All captured fish immediately were placed in plastic buckets filled with ambient stream water and air bubblers. Captured fish were anesthetized with the smallest possible dose of MS-222 before handling. After the fish recovered, they were released back to their approximate point of capture. The exception to this protocol was when a fish died before or during handling. Dead fish were placed on ice and transported to the U.S. Fish and Wildlife Service's Lower Columbia River Fish Health Center (LCRFHC) for disease profiling.

All captured fish were identified, scanned for passive integrated transponder tags (PIT tags), measured for fork length (FL) to the nearest millimeter, weighed to the nearest 0.1 g, and inspected for external signs of disease. Tissue samples (fin clip) from a subsample of salmonids were preserved in 95 percent ethanol and archived for future genetic analyses (not funded as of 2012). To mark each fish for tracking movements and measuring growth, we inserted PIT tags (12 mm; 134.2 kHz) in the peritoneal cavity of trout that exceeded 70-mm FL. All PIT-tagging followed the procedures outlined by the Columbia Basin Fish and Wildlife Authority (1999). All PIT-tag data were entered in the PIT Tag Integration System database, which is maintained by Pacific States Marine Fisheries Commission. To mark all trout that are less than 70 mm FL, we clipped a small part of the upper caudal fin during the first electrofishing pass in each reach, each year. During the recapture pass, unmarked trout exceeding 70 mm FL were PIT-tagged, but unmarked trout less than 70 mm FL were returned to the stream unmarked. We attempted to capture all observed salmonids and a subset of any other fish species observed while electrofishing to determine fish species composition in each reach.

For our mark-recapture data analysis, we estimated the number of age-0 trout (<80 mm FL) and age-1 or older trout (>80 mm FL) as follows:

$$N = [(M + 1)*(C + 1)/ R + 1] - 1, \qquad (2)$$

Where

> M = number of fish marked on the first sample,
> C = number of fish captured in the second sample, and
> R = number of marked fish captured in the second sample (Chapman, 1951).

The confidence interval for each estimate was calculated using a normal approximation, however, we used a binomial distribution when R/C was greater than 0.10 (Seber, 1982).

The fish received by the LCRFHC were inspected rigorously for disease. Diseases screened at the LCRFHC by testing or microscopic observations included bacterial agents (bacterial kidney disease, coldwater disease, columnaris, emphysematous putrefactive disease, furunculosis, and enteric redmouth), viral agents (infectious pancreatic necrosis, infectious hematopoietic necrosis, and viral hemorrhagic septicemia), and parasitic agents (whirling disease, *Ceratomyxa*, digenetic trematodes, *Myxobolus kisutchi*, *Myxidium minteri*, *Hexamita*, *Gyrodactulus*, *Scyphidia*, and *Heteropolaria*).

The results of the habitat and fish surveys in this report were compared with the EDT model attribute rankings outlined in Allen and Connolly (2005). Model inputs were rated based on EDT attribute rating guidelines (Lestelle and others, 2004). We included the model inputs in the sections, "Results of Survey" and "Discussion of Findings" where the revised attribute rating, based on the data collected for this report, were not consistent with the attribute ratings used to characterize Buck Creek in Allen and Connolly (2005). No additional EDT model runs were conducted as part of this study.

Results of Surveys

Habitat Results

We found Buck Creek to be confined, with a single straight channel, low sinuosity, and an average gradient of 3.6 percent (table 2). The gradient was lowest in Reach 1 (1.1 percent) and highest in Reach 3 (4.0 percent; table 2). Confinement ratio (width of the valley floodplain divided by bankfull channel width) ranged from 1.1 in Reaches 1 and 2 to 1.6 in Reach 4 (table 2). Large-cobble riffles were 83 percent of the available habitat overall. Pools were rare, comprising 15 percent of the overall surface area (table 2). Where we had permission to survey, Reach 1 had only one pool, so any summary of pools in this reach was for that pool only. In Reaches 2, 3, and 4, pools mostly were formed by bedrock and were relatively simple and shallow, with a mean residual pool depth of 32 cm. Mean instream and overhead cover for fish was similar between reaches and was low (29 percent; table 3). About one-half (14 of 29 percent) of the instream cover for fish was provided by interstitial spaces in the cobble and boulders. Mean overhead cover did not exceed a few percent (table 3). Stream shading was highest in Reach 4 (mean of 65 percent) and 90 percent was from deciduous vegetation (table 2).

Boulders (64 percent) and large cobble (23 percent) were the dominant stream substrate (table 4). Potential spawning substrate of small cobble and gravel comprised only 6 percent of the dominant substrate type averaged across all 100-m transects. Spawning gravel cores were not able to be obtained, owing to large substrate distributed within the small sites with spawning gravel. This suggests that spawning habitat is of low quality and abundance. Substrate embeddedness (2.7 percent) and percent fines (11 percent) were highest in the 200 m of Reach 1 that we had permission to survey (table 4).

The inner riparian zone (0–3 m from bankfull width) was dominated by small-diameter alder (*Alnus rubra*) (figs. 2– 5). However, coniferous vegetation typically dominated the outer riparian canopy (3–10 m from bankfull width), being most common in Reach 4 (fig. 5). Several transects in Reach 1 had no riparian trees, largely because of clearing for lawns, cabins, or roads (fig. 2). The riparian forest transects surveyed in Reach 2 had several coniferous trees with diameters at breast height up to 100 cm, which was larger than the other reaches (fig. 3). There was abundant evidence of historical conifer removal within the riparian area. More than 60 large-diameter (generally greater than 100 cm) cedar stumps with cut ends were noted in the riparian areas of Reaches 2, 3, and 4; however these trees are not evident as LWD in the stream.

Instream wood (>10 cm diameter, >2 m length) averaged 7 pieces per 100 m (table 5), 80 percent of which was less than 50 cm in diameter at midpoint, which is the TFW and EDT standard for "large" or "key" LWD (fig. 6). Overall, the LWD averaged 33 cm in diameter and 6

8

m in length, with few differences between reaches (table 5). The composition of LWD was increasingly coniferous in the upper reaches and averaged 51 percent coniferous over all reaches. The distribution of LWD was uneven, with 38 percent of the 20-m intervals over all reaches containing no LWD. Few pieces of LWD were storing sediment (33 percent) or forming pools (12 percent, table 5). Key LWD pieces (>50 cm in diameter) were more abundant in Reaches 3 and 4 (table 5). Key LWD pieces were more likely to be sediment-storing or pool-forming, with 73 percent of these pieces having at least one of these functions (5 of 8 in Reach 2, 10 of 17 in Reach 3, and 16 of 18 in Reach 4).

Water temperature at the Buck Creek temperature recording sites did not exceed 18 °C in 2009 or 2010 (table 6). The maximum temperature recorded was 17.2 °C in Reach 1 on August 2, 2009 (table 6). The temperatures did not exceed 16 °C in 2010; however, the latest date that data were available in Reach 1 was on July 5, 2010 (the thermograph was buried in substrate and lost), and the warmest stream temperatures were likely in late July or early August. Water temperatures in 2009 were warmer than in 2010, with more days when temperatures exceeded 14 °C in Reaches 2 and 3. The thermograph in Reach 4 was covered by a fallen log, and the data were not recovered. Mean daily temperatures were similar between reaches but were consistently higher in Reach 1 during the summer months (fig. 7).

Within a given date at the sites where we measured discharge, there was always less in Reach 2 than in Reach 3 (fig. 8). The lowest measured summer discharge in Buck Creek was 3.3 ft^3/s in Reach 2 downstream of the irrigation diversion at rkm 3.1 (fig. 8; table 7). The lowest measured discharge was 8.7 ft^3/s in Reach 3 and 7.7 ft^3/s in Reach 1 (rkm 0.2) (table 7). The greatest difference in discharge between Reaches 2 and 3 was 8.1 ft^3/s on July 10, 2009, and the smallest difference between these reaches was 2.0 ft^3/s on October 5, 2010.

Macroinvertebrate collections and assessment using the B-IBI indicated that Buck Creek macroinvertebrate species diversity and, therefore, water quality was good in Reaches 1 and 2, and excellent in Reaches 3 and 4, according to the B-IBI (table 8). The primary difference in the invertebrate community was a lower percentage of predator species and a higher percentage of tolerant taxa in Reaches 1 and 2 (table 8).

Data collected during the habitat survey suggest that 15 of the EDT model attributes could be revised based on this more thorough survey (table 9). Although many of the attribute revisions are small changes, a few are large enough to likely change the model outputs. In particular, the percentages of each habitat type in each reach substantially differed from those in the original model inputs (table 9). For example, we found almost no small cobble riffles; however, the original model input had small cobble riffles as 9 percent of the total habitat type. We also found only half (10 percent) of the amount of pool habitat compared to the original model inputs (20 percent pool, table 9). We do not know how much the model outputs would change if the suggested revisions were included. However, if additional EDT model runs are conducted, we believe that the revised attribute values would better reflect the conditions in Buck Creek in 2010.

Fish Results

Rainbow trout and shorthead sculpin *(Cottus confusus)* were the only fish species present in all reaches. Brook lamprey *(Lampetra richardsonii),* longnose dace *(Rhinichthys cataractae),* and brook trout *(Salvelinus fontinalis)* were found only in Reach 1 (table 10). Large Pacific giant salamanders *(Dicamptodon tenebrosus)* commonly were seen in all reaches. The length of stream that was electrofished to obtain population estimates varied by reach and year. In Reach 1, the sampling distance was bounded by the confluence with the White Salmon River and an upstream property boundary. The sampling distances in Reaches 2, 3, and 4 was longer in 2009, with sections of about 200 m sampled in 2010 (tables 11 and 12). During electrofishing surveys in 2009, we handled 1,127 rainbow trout, 451 of which we PIT tagged. During electrofishing surveys in 2010, we handled 910 rainbow trout, 249 of which we PIT tagged. Age-0 rainbow trout were present in all reaches in 2009 and 2010, indicating successful recruitment in all reaches. The greatest abundance of age-0 rainbow trout was in Reach 1 in both 2009 and 2010, with more than twice the abundance of any other reach (fig. 9). There was a trend of decreasing abundance of age-0 trout going from downstream to upstream, although fish abundance or biomass per meter was not significantly different among reaches for age-0 trout or age-1 and older trout (Analysis of Variance or ANOVA, $P>0.05$).

Mean annual growth rates of fish tagged at ages 1 and 2 (80–158 mm FL) were similar between reaches (fig. 10) and averaged 28 mm and 17 g over all reaches. Although mean annual growth rates were lowest in Reach 2 (fig. 10), there was no statistical difference in annual growth rates of PIT-tagged fish between reaches (ANOVA, $P>0.05$). However, given the variability in the growth of individual fish, the sample size of fish tagged in 2009 that were recaptured in 2010 (1 in Reach 1, 13 in Reach 2, 7 in Reach 3, and 9 in Reach 4) was likely insufficient to have the statistical power to detect growth differences between reaches if they exist. The greatest annual increase in FL of an individual PIT-tagged fish was 51 mm for a fish tagged at 82 mm FL in Reach 2. The length-frequency distribution of age-0 trout in Reach 1 ranged from 32 mm to 86 mm FL in 2009 and 2010, and was wider than that of the other reaches. By inferring the age based on the length-frequency histograms, the longest age-0 trout was 72 mm FL in Reach 2 in 2009, and 68 mm FL in the other reaches (figs. 11–14). In 2009 and 2010, the largest trout were captured in Reach 4—247 mm (fig. 12) and 235 mm (fig. 14), respectively. Nearly all recaptured fish were tagged in the same reach the previous year, indicating little movement of fish between reaches. However, fish may have moved and returned between sampling periods, and fish that outmigrated from Buck Creek likely would not be recaptured. One known example of outmigration from Buck Creek was a rainbow trout (tagged at 97 mm FL in Reach 3 on July 21, 2009) that was detected at the Bonneville Dam juvenile bypass facility on May 16, 2011. This fish was tagged at age 1, and migrated towards the ocean, presumably as an age-3 smolt, indicating that some anadromous life history potential exists in the Buck Creek rainbow trout population.

Trout in Buck Creek generally were in good health. A total of 23 rainbow trout were submitted to the LCRFHC for disease assessments from the three lower reaches of Buck Creek on five sampling dates in 2010. One fish from Reach 1 was confirmed by LCRFHC to have bacterial kidney disease (BKD), *Renibacterium salmoninarum*. We noted copepods on fish fins and gills in all reaches in 2009 and 2010, with the highest incidence in Reach 2 (7 fish with copepods in 2009 and 8 fish with copepods in 2010). We found suspected *Epistylis*, a parasitic ciliate, on one fish in Reach 2. Otherwise, the fish appeared to be in good health and LCRFHC did not detect any other bacterial, viral, or parasitic agents.

Discussion of Findings

We found Buck Creek to be confined and incised, with a single straight channel and low sinuosity. Although this may be a natural condition owing to the valley shape and steep topography, it is possible that, as was the case with many neighboring streams and rivers, Buck Creek was historically used to transport harvested timber, experienced active wood removal from the stream, or both, because very little instream wood remains compared to likely historical conditions. Although we could not find documentation that splash damming, log driving, or "stream cleaning" (the removal of instream LWD) occurred in Buck Creek, we suspect, given habitat conditions at the time of the survey, that this stream underwent one or more of these processes that were typical of past logging practices. Instream wood averaged 0.4–0.9 pieces per channel width (6–10 pieces per 100 m) and most (80 percent) were less than 50 cm in diameter. In an unmanaged drainage basin, a typical stream of this size and gradient would have 2–2.5 pieces per channel width, with a greater proportion of pieces greater than 50 cm in diameter (Peterson and others, 1992). Much of the instream LWD that we observed was derived from alder and other hardwood species, which degrade faster and are less effective geomorphic agents compared to conifers (Hyatt and Naiman, 2001).

Large-cobble riffles constituted most of the available overall habitat. Boulders and cobble dominated the stream substrate, with limited spawning gravel. Pools, totaling 15 percent of the overall surface area, mostly were formed by bedrock, with little instream cover and low complexity. In comparable basins where riparian timber had been removed, numerous studies have found less instream LWD and pool habitat compared to unmanaged drainage basins (Ralph and others, 1994; Montgomery and others, 1995). Individual LWD pieces are often a major component of pool-forming features in forested streams (Montgomery and others, 1995). Where LWD is less abundant, there tend to be fewer pools, longer riffles, and less structural complexity, gravel retention, and sediment sorting (Ralph and others, 1994; Dolloff and Warren, 2003). This reduction in habitat quality often results in reduced fish abundance and smaller individual fish (Dolloff and Warren, 2003). In Buck Creek, the reduction in pool habitats will likely favor rainbow trout and steelhead, which are better adapted to use riffle habitats, over recolonizing coho, which are more dependent on pool habitats (Bisson and others, 1988). Restoration of LWD quantities to levels approaching PFC would likely benefit all salmonid species.

Water temperatures did not exceed 18 °C in any of the study reaches. Water temperature in Buck Creek rarely exceeded 16 °C and did so only in the lowest reach in 2009, although the thermograph in Reach 1 could not be recovered in 2010 and may have exceeded 16 °C in that year as well. Water temperatures were within the optimal growth range for salmon and trout, which is 10–15 °C (assuming food is limited) (U.S. Environmental Protection Agency, 2003). Optimum feeding temperature for rainbow trout is between 13 and 16 °C (Cherry and others, 1975; Kaya and others, 1977). The water temperatures in Buck Creek were substantially cooler than those in Rattlesnake Creek (a nearby tributary to the White Salmon River), which were much greater than the optimal temperatures and in some locations approached 24 °C (Allen and others, 2006). At temperatures greater than 20°C, rainbow trout can experience high metabolic demands and stress, which can lead to suppressed growth and increased early mortality (Hokanson and others, 1977; Nielsen and others, 1994). At temperatures greater than 24°C, high mortalities can occur (Cherry and others, 1975). However, even with the warmer water temperatures in Rattlesnake Creek, the trout abundance (ranging from 0.3 to 0.5 age-1 or older trout/m) (Allen and others, 2006) was similar to that of Buck Creek (ranging from 0.4 to 0.9 age-1 or older trout/m).There were numerous springs in Buck Creek, particularly upstream of the study reaches, that contributed to maintaining cool water temperatures throughout the summer. The gradient, summer discharge, incised stream channel, and canopy shading also contributed to maintaining cool water temperatures.

Water discharge in Reach 4 of Buck Creek always was equal to or greater than 7 ft^3/s during summer 2009 and 2010. However, the city of White Salmon was not operating its municipal water diversion until late July 2010. Water discharge was as low as 3.3 ft^3/s in Reach 2 on September 15, 2009 (table 7). On this same day, water discharge was 9.6 ft^3/s in Reach 3 about 300 m upstream of the measurement in Reach 2. This decrease in discharge, likely owing to water withdrawal at the irrigation diversion, may account for the reduction in annual growth of rainbow trout in Reach 2 compared to the reaches upstream. However, this reduced annual growth also may be attributed to small sample size or other environmental factors. Some of the discrepancy in discharge between Reaches 2 and 3 could be due to unaccounted-for differences in hyporheic flow between the two measuring sites. Discharge could not be measured in the irrigation ditch to further quantify differences in discharge due to lack of permission for access.

Water quality in Buck Creek was considered good-to-excellent, based on the B-IBI scores. The variety and types of macroinvertebrate species that were collected show that the water chemistry, flow regime, turbidity, and fine sediment were not impaired substantially during the surveys in Buck Creek. However, the B-IBI scores are progressively lower from samples taken farther downstream; suggesting that overall stream health is reduced in Reaches 1 and 2. The Underwood Conservation District measured general water chemistry (pH, conductivity, turbidity, dissolved oxygen, and temperature), and advanced laboratory water chemistry (total phosphorus, nitrate and nitrite as nitrogen, and total suspended solids) from 2001 through 2005, and also found Buck Creek to have good water quality (White and Cochran, 2005). This is not surprising, as Buck Creek is the municipal water supply for the city of White Salmon.

Rainbow trout was the dominant fish species in Buck Creek, and there was evidence of recruitment in all reaches. The greatest abundance of age-0 rainbow trout (8 fish/m in 2009, and 4 fish/m in 2010) was in the most downstream reach. This may be because of larger trout from the White Salmon River, which typically have more eggs, using Buck Creek as a spawning tributary, due to age-0 fish that hatched from upstream areas migrating into and rearing in the lower 200 m of Buck Creek, or due to high egg-to-fry survival in Reach 1. Because trout fry typically move downstream to rear after hatching (Quinn, 2005), the decreasing abundance in age-0 trout in the upstream reaches also may be due to increasing gradient and cumulatively less spawning gravel and fewer spawning trout in the upstream reaches. Reach 1 in Buck Creek had the most fish species diversity, likely because it is near the White Salmon River. It is unlikely that brook trout have a persistent population spawning in Buck Creek because only a few individuals were found, and those found were near the confluence with the White Salmon River.

Rainbow trout found in Buck Creek had relatively high growth rates and low disease prevalence. The average annual growth rates of age-1 or older trout of 26 mm in Reaches 2 and 4, and 35 mm in Reach 3, were slightly lower than the average annual growth rates in Rattlesnake Creek (ranging from 30 to 41 mm, depending on the reach) (Allen and others, 2006). This may be due to warmer temperatures in Rattlesnake Creek increasing metabolism and, therefore, growth of fish, assuming adequate food resources.

There were a few EDT parameters whose values changed enough to potentially alter the model outputs for Buck Creek. The changes most likely to influence the outputs are the percentages of stream habitat types. We found substantially less pool habitat, and more large-cobble riffle habitat, compared with the original model inputs. The stream also is more naturally confined than originally modeled. These changes would likely reduce the modeled estimates of productivity and abundance of salmonids in Buck Creek. This, in turn, would elevate the potential restoration value of the Buck Creek reaches because they are more degraded from pristine conditions than originally concluded by Allen and Connolly (2005), using the EDT model.

After the restoration of fish passage in the White Salmon River downstream of the confluence with Buck Creek, rainbow trout will be able to express all of their potential life histories. These life histories include residency, potadromy, and anadromy (Northcote, 1997). Resident and anadromous *O. mykiss* co-exist in many Pacific Northwest drainages (Scott and Crossman, 1973). Along with the increased opportunities for life-history expression, the rainbow trout may experience introgression or competition from steelhead straying from other basins. These Buck Creek trout also may encounter newly recolonizing coho salmon, Chinook salmon, Pacific lamprey, and bull trout. It is our intention that, along with aiding in the prioritization of restoration needs, this report will provide a baseline to which future fish populations and habitat conditions can be compared as anadromous fish have a chance to recolonize.

Acknowledgments

We would like to thank Cara Holem, Teresa Fish, Christy Barszewski, and Jessica Fischer of the USGS for all their hard work collecting data in the field. We would like to thank Todd Olson and PacifiCorp for permission to sample on PacifiCorp's property. We appreciate stream temperature data provided by Tova Tillinghast (Underwood Conservation District) and Greg Morris (Yakama Nation). Greg Morris also provided benthic invertebrate samples for B-IBI analysis and a McNeil core sampler for use on this project. We would like to thank Ian Jezorek (USGS) and John Foltz (Klickitat County) for thoughtful reviews of this report.

References Cited

Allen, M.B., and Connolly, P.J., 2005, Assessment of the White Salmon watershed using the ecosystem diagnosis and treatment model: U.S. Geological Survey, Columbia River Research Laboratory, Cook, Washington, 55 p.

Allen, M.B., Connolly, P.J., Jezorek, I.G., Munz, C., and Charrier, J.C., 2006, Assess current and potential salmonid production in Rattlesnake Creek in association with restoration efforts: U.S. Geological Survey 2004–2005 Annual Report, Project No. 200102500, BPA Report DOE/BP-00005068-4, 101 p.

Aspect Consulting, 2011, City of White Salmon aquifer storage and recovery feasibility assessment: Prepared for the city of White Salmon, Washington, Project No. 090094-001-03, 130 p., accessed November 16, 2012, at *http://www.ecy.wa.gov/programs/wr/cwp/images/pdf/wsasr_final4-22-11.pdf*.

Bain, M.B., and Stevenson, N.J., 1999, Aquatic habitat assessment—Common methods: American Fisheries Society, Bethesda, Maryland, 216 p.

Beechie, T.J., and Bolton, S., 1999, An approach to restoring salmonid habitat-forming processes in Pacific Northwest watersheds: Fisheries, v. 24, no. 4, p. 6–15.

Bisson, P.A., Nielsen, J.L., Palmason, R.A., and Grove, L.E., 1982, A system of naming habitat types in small streams, with examples of habitat utilization by salmonids during low streamflow, *in* Armantrout, N.B., ed., Acquisition and utilization of aquatic habitat inventory information symposium: Bethesda, Maryland, American Fisheries Society, Western Division, , p. 62–73.

Bisson, P.A, Sullivan, K., and Nielsen, J.L., 1988, Channel hydraulics, habitat use, and body form of juvenile coho salmon, steelhead, and cutthroat trout in streams: Transactions of the North American Fisheries Society, v. 117, p. 262–273.

Busby, P.J., Wainwright, T.C., Bryant, G.J., Lierheimer, L.J., Waples, R.S., Waknitz, F.W., and Lagomarsino, I.V., 1996, Status review of west coast steelhead from Washington, Idaho, Oregon, and California: U.S. Department of Commerce, National Oceanic and Atmospheric Administration Tech. Memo. NMFS-NWFSC-27, 261 p.

Chapman, D.G., 1951, Some properties of the hypergeometric distribution with applications to zoological sample censuses: University of California Publications in Statistics, v. 1, p. 131–160.

Cherry, D.S., Dickson, K.L., and Cairns, J., Jr., 1975, Temperatures selected and avoided by fish at various acclimation temperatures: Journal of the Fisheries Research Board of Canada, v. 32, p. 485–491.

Columbia Basin Fish and Wildlife Authority, 1999, PIT Tag Marking Procedures Manual: Portland, Oregon, Columbia Basin Fish and Wildlife Authority, PIT Tag Steeping Committee, 26 p.

Dolloff, C.A., and Warren, M.L., Jr., 2003, Fish relationships with wood in small streams, *in* Gregory, S.V., Boyer, K.L., and Gurnell, A.M., eds., The Ecology and management of wood in world rivers: American Fisheries Society, Symposium 37, Bethesda, Maryland, p. 179–194.

Feist, B.E., Steel, E.A., Pess, G.R., and Bilby, R.E., 2003, The influence of scale on salmon habitat restoration priorities: Animal Conservation, v. 6, p. 271–282.

Fore, L.S., Karr, J.R., and Wisseman, R.W., 1996, Assessing invertebrate responses to human activities—Evaluating alternative approaches: Journal of the North American Benthological Society, v. 15, p. 212–231.

Hall, J.D., and Baker, C.O., 1982, Rehabilitating and enhancing stream habitat—1. Review and evaluation, chap. 12. *of* Meehan, W.R. eds. Influence of forest and rangeland management on anadromous fish habitat in western North America: U.S. Department of Agriculture, Forest Service, Pacific Northwest Research Station, Gen. Tech. Rep. PNW-138, Portland, Oregon.

Hokanson, K.E., Kleiner, C.F., and Thorslund, T.W., 1977, Effects of constant temperatures and diel temperature fluctuations on specific growth and mortality rates and yield of juvenile rainbow trout, *Salmo gairdneri*: Journal of Fisheries Research Board of Canada, v. 34, p. 639–648.

Hyatt, T.L., and Naiman, R.J., 2001, The residence time of large woody debris in the Queets River, Washington, USA: Ecological Applications, v. 11, p. 191–202.

Karr, J.R., 1998, Rivers as sentinels: using the biology of rivers to guide landscape management, *in* Naiman, R.J. and Bilby, B.E., eds.: River ecology and management—Lessons from the Pacific coastal ecoregion: New York, Springer-Verlag, p. 502–528.

Karr, J.R., Fausch, K.D., Angermeier, P.L., Yant, P.R., and Schlosser, I. J., 1986, Assessing biological integrity in running waters—A method and its rationale: Illinois Natural History Survey, Special Publication 5, Champaign, Illinois. 31 p.

Kaya, C.M., Kaeding L.R., and Burkhalter, D.E., 1977, Use of a cold-water refuge by rainbow and brown trout in a geothermally heated stream: Progressive Fish-Culturist, v. 39, p. 37–39.

Kleindl, W.J., 1995, A benthic index of biotic integrity for Puget Sound lowland streams, Washington, USA: Seattle, University of Washington, M.S. thesis.

Lestelle, L.C., Mobrand, L.E., and McConnaha, W.E., 2004, Information structure of ecosystem diagnosis and treatment (EDT) and habitat rating rules for Chinook salmon, coho salmon, and steelhead trout: Mobrand Biometrics Inc., Vashon, Washington, accessed November 16, 2012, at *http://www.mobrand.com/MBI/pdfs/EDT%20InfoStructure_ChinCohoStlhd_June2004.pdf.*

Mobrand L.E., 2002, Subbasin planning with EDT—A primer: Mobrand Biometrics, Inc. Vashon, Washington, accessed November 16, 2012, at *http://www.mobrand.com/MBI/pdfs/Subbasin_planning.pdf.*

Montgomery, D.R., Buffington, J.M., Smith, R.D., Schmidt, K.M., and Pess, George., 1995, Pool spacing in forest channels: Water Resources Research v. 31, p. 1097–1105.

Morley, S. A. 2000. Effects of urbanization on the biological integrity of Puget Sound lowland streams—Restoration with a biological focus: Seattle, University of Washington, M.S. thesis, accessed November 16, 2012, at *http://depts.washington.edu/cuwrm/.*

National Marine Fisheries Service, 2005, Final listing determinations for 16 ESUs of West Coast Salmon, and final 4(d) protective regulations for threatened salmonid ESUs: Federal Register. v. 70, no. 123, p. 37160–37204, June 28, 2005.

Nielsen, J.L., Lisle, T.E., and Ozaki, V., 1994, Thermally stratified pools and their use by steelhead in northern California streams: Transactions of the American Fisheries Society, v. 123, p. 613–626.

Normandeau and Associates, 2004, White Salmon Subbasin plan: Prepared for the Northwest Power and Conservation Council, Portland, Oregon, 248 p.

Northcote, T.G., 1997, Potadromy, *in* Salomidae–Living and moving in the fast lane: North American Journal of Fisheries Management, v. 17, p. 1029–1045.

Peterson, N.P., Hendry, A., and Quinn, T.P., 1992, Assessment of cumulative effects on salmonid habitat—Some suggested parameters and target conditions: Prepared for the Washington State Department of Natural Resources under the Timber, Fish, and Wildlife Agreement, TFW-F3-92-001, March, 78 p.

Pleus, A.E., Schuett-Hames, D., and Bullchild L., 1999, TFW monitoring program method manual for the habitat unit survey: Prepared for the Washington State Department of Natural Resources under the Timber, Fish, and Wildlife Agreement, TFW-AM9-99-003, DNR No. 105, June.

Plummer, E., and Zuckerman, A., 2011, White Salmon River watershed anadromous fish passage inventory 2009–2011 survey report: Underwood Conservation District, White Salmon, Washington, 53 p.

Prichard, D., Barrett, H., Cagney, J., Clark, R., Fogg, J., Gebhardt, K., Hansen, .P, Mitchell, B., and Tippy, D., 1993, Riparian area management: process for assessing proper functioning condition—Technical Reference 1737-9: Bureau of Land Management, BLM/SC/ST-93/003+1737, Denver, Colorado.

Puget Sound Stream Benthos, 2012a, Puget Sound Stream Benthos Monitoring and Analysis: website, accessed December 17, 2012, at http://pugetsoundstreambenthos.org/Default.aspx.

Puget Sound Stream Benthos, 2012b, Benthic taxa attributes: website, accessed December 17, 2012, at http://pugetsoundstreambenthos.org/Taxa-Attributes.aspx.

Quinn, T.P., 2005, The behavior and ecology of Pacific salmon and trout: Seattle, University of Washington Press, 378 p.

Raleigh, R.F., Hickman, T., Solomon, R.C., and Nelson, P.C, 1984, Habitat suitability information—Rainbow trout: U.S. Fish and Wildlife Service, FWS/OBS-82/10.60. 64 p.

Ralph, S.C., Poole, G.C., Conquest, L.L., and Naiman, R.J., 1994, Stream channel morphology and woody debris in logged and unlogged basins of western Washington: Canadian Journal of Fisheries and Aquatic Sciences v. 51, p. 37–51.

Rosenfeld, Jordan, 2003, Assessing the habitat requirements of stream fishes—An overview and evaluation of different approaches: Transactions of the North American Fisheries Society, v. 132, p. 953–968.

Scott, W.B., and Crossman, E.J., 1973, Freshwater fishes of Canada (5th ed., 1990): Ottawa, Fisheries Research Board of Canada, p. 327–332.

Schuett-Hames, D., Conrad, R., Pleus, A.E., and McHenry, M., 1999b, TFW monitoring program method manual for the salmonid spawning gravel composition survey: Prepared for the Washington State Department of Natural Resources under the Timber, Fish, and Wildlife Agreement, TFW-AM9-99-001, DNR no. 101, March.

Schuett-Hames, D., Pleus, A.E., and Smith, D., 1999a, TFW monitoring program method manual for the salmonid spawning habitat availability survey: Prepared for the Washington State Department of Natural Resources under the Timber, Fish, and Wildlife Agreement, TFW-AM9-99-007, DNR no. 109, November.

Schuett-Hames, D., Pleus, A.E., Ward, J., Fox, M., and Light, J., 1999c, TFW monitoring program method manual for the large woody debris survey: Prepared for the Washington State Department of Natural Resources under the Timber, Fish, and Wildlife Agreement, TFW-AM9-99-004, DNR no. 106.

Seber, G.A.F., 1982, The estimation of animal abundance and related parameters (2d ed.): New York, Macmillan.

Temple, G.M., and Pearsons, T.N., 2007, Electrofishing—Backpack and drift boat, *in* Johnson, D.H., Shrier, B.M., O'Neal, J.S., Knutzen, J.A., Augerot, X., O'Neil, T.A., and Pearsons, T.N., eds., Salmonid field protocols handbook—Techniques for assessing status and trends in salmon and trout populations: Bethesda, Maryland, American Fisheries Society, p. 95–132.

U.S. Environmental Protection Agency, 2003, EPA Region 10 guidance for Pacific Northwest state and tribal temperature water quality standards: U.S. Environmental Protection Agency, Office of Water, Region 10, Seattle, Washington, EPA 910-B-03-002.

White, Jim, and Cochrane, Tova, 2005, Assess current and potential salmonid production in Rattlesnake Creek associated with restoration efforts: Underwood Conservation District, 2004–2005 Annual Report, Project No. 200102500, BPA Report DOE/BP-00006301-4, 31 p.

Williams, J.E., Wood, C.A., and Dombeck, M.P., 1997, Watershed restoration—Principles and practices: Bethesda, Maryland, American Fisheries Society.

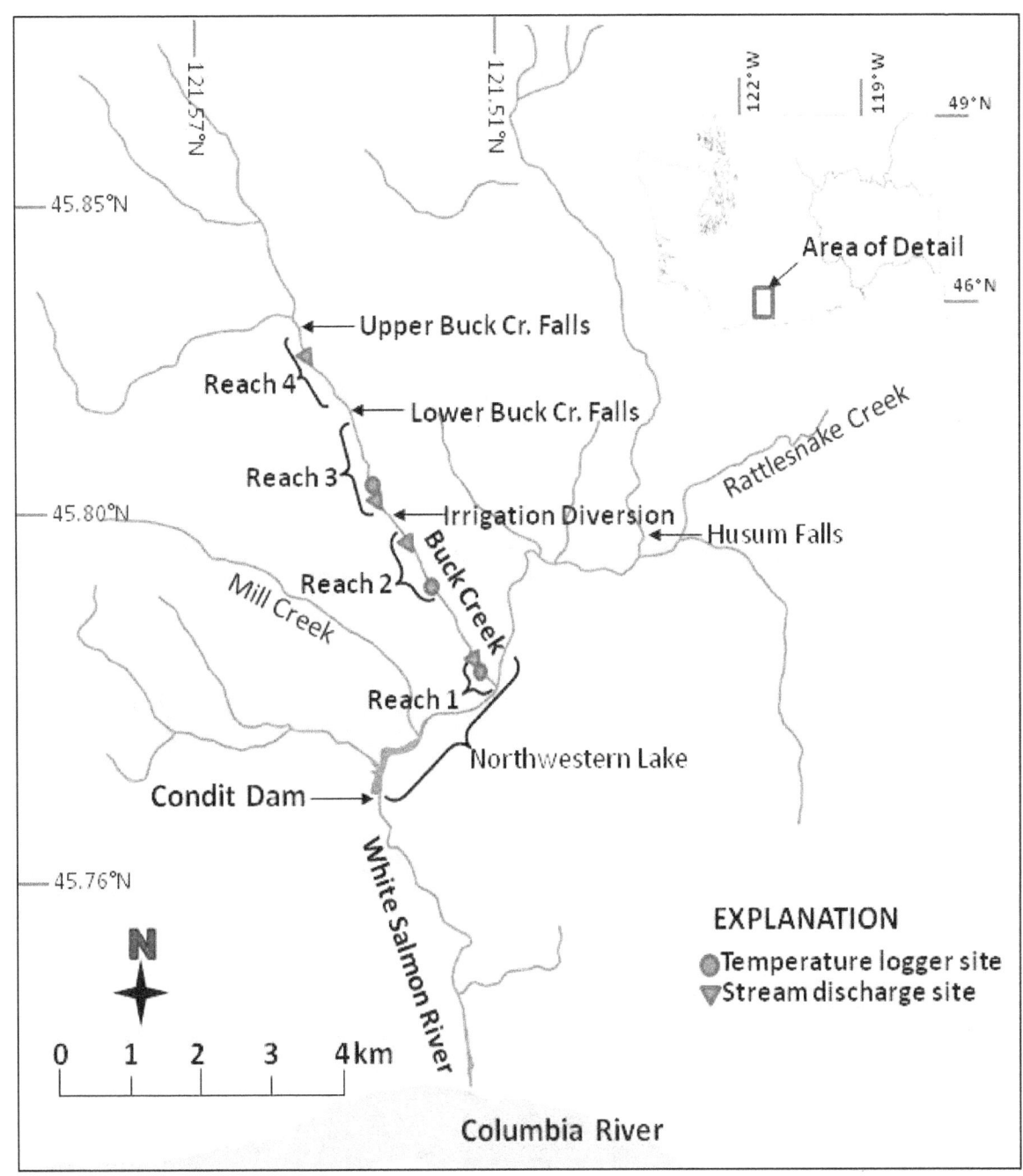

Figure 1. Map of Buck Creek, study reaches, waterfalls, and irrigation diversions within the White Salmon River basin, Washington.

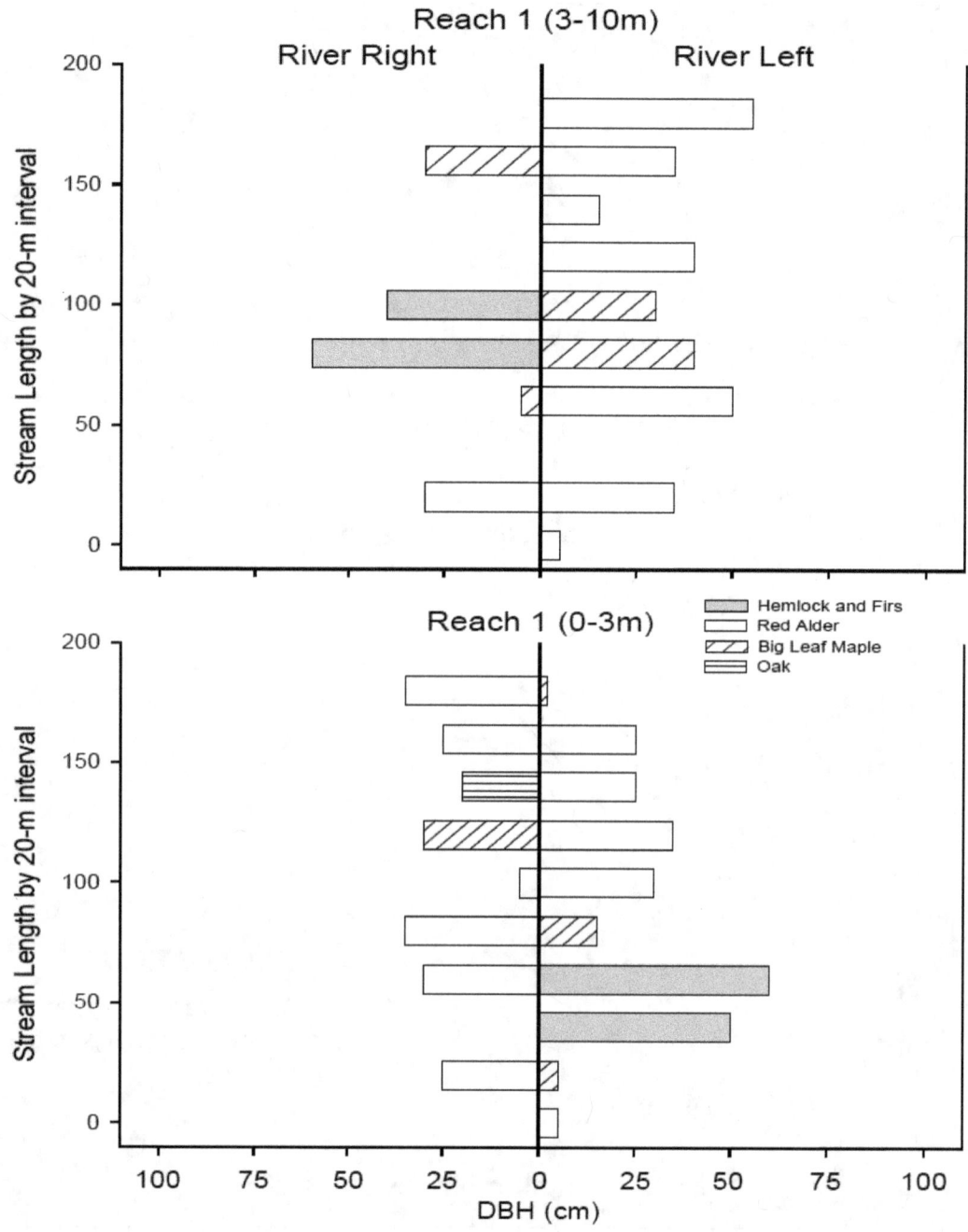

Figure 2. Characterization of outer (3–10 meters from bankfull) and adjacent (0–3 meters from bankfull) riparian vegetation in Reach 1 of Buck Creek, Washington (river kilometers 0–0.2). The diameter at breast height (DBH) of the dominant tree type within a 10-meter section at each 20-meter transect is shown. Blanks indicate the lack of canopy-height trees (approximately greater than 3 meters tall) within the 10-meter section.

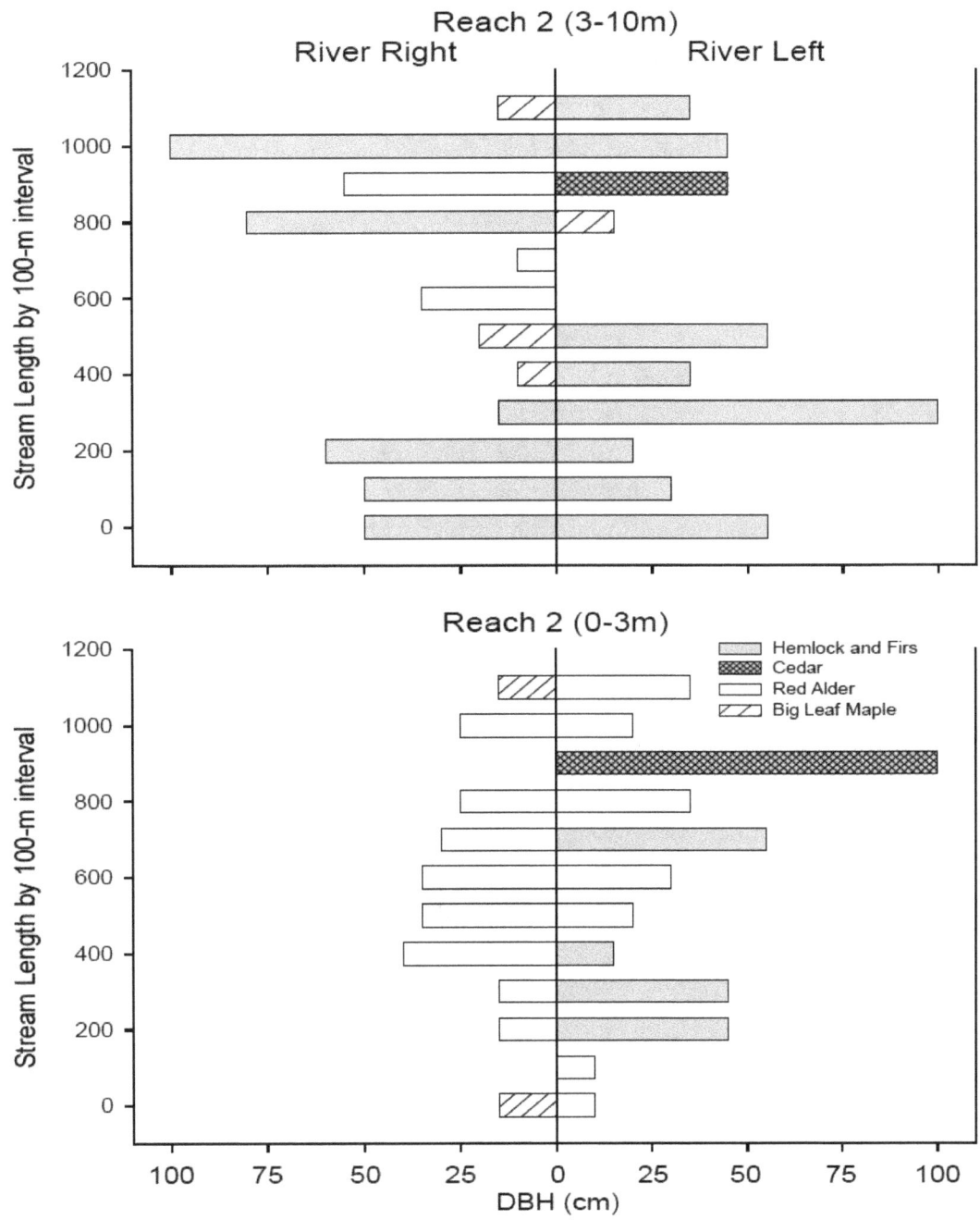

Figure 3. Characterization of outer (3–10 meters from bankfull) and adjacent (0–3 meters from bankfull) riparian vegetation in Reach 2 of Buck Creek, Washington (river kilometers 2.0–3.1). The diameter at breast height (DBH) of the dominant tree type within a 10-meter section at each 20-meter transect is shown. Blanks indicate the lack of canopy-height trees (approximately greater than 3 meters tall) within the 10-meter section.

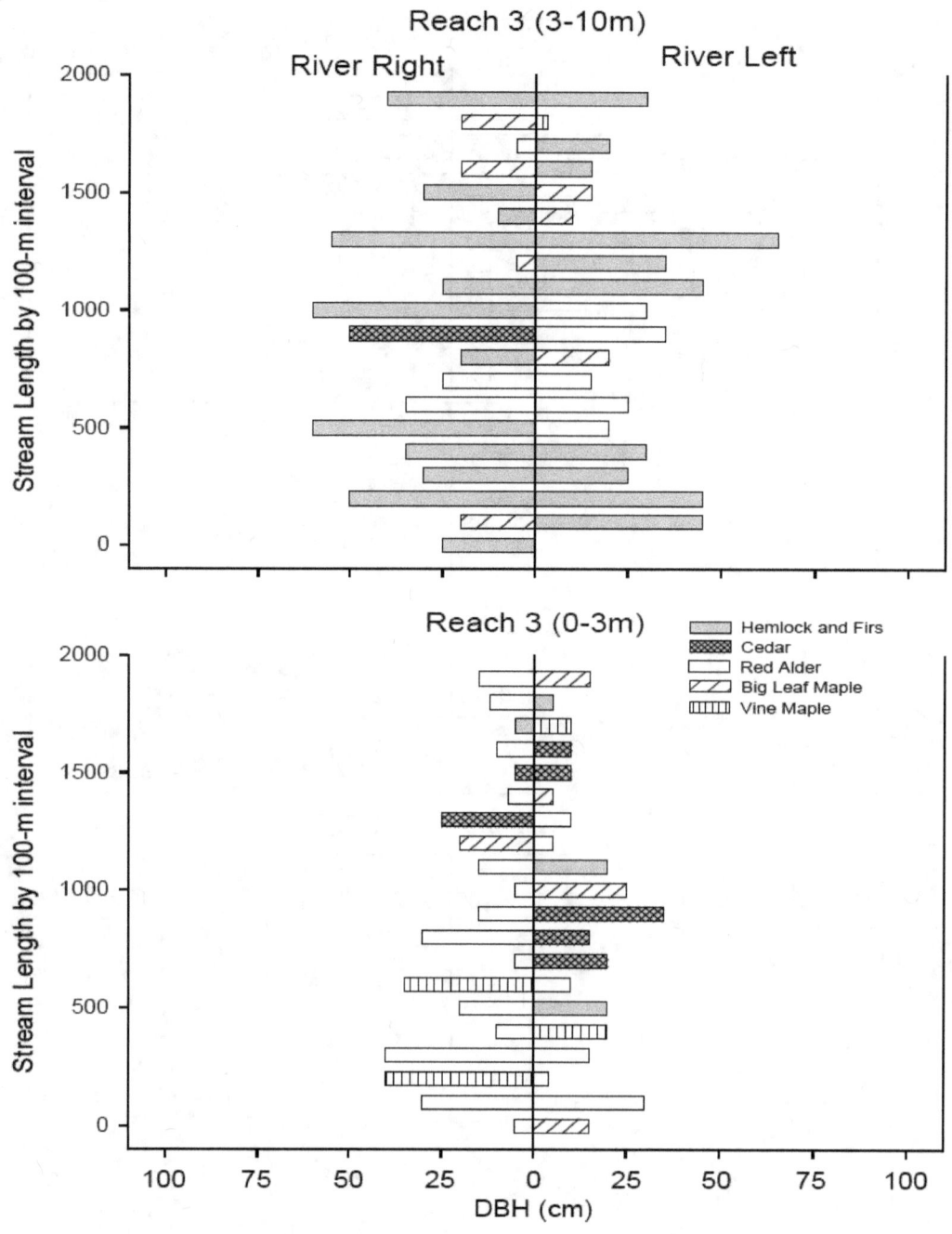

Figure 4. Characterization of outer (3–10 meters from bankfull) and adjacent (0–3 meters from bankfull) riparian vegetation in Reach 3 of Buck Creek, Washington (river kilometers 3.1–5.0). The diameter at breast height (DBH) of the dominant tree type within a 10-meter section at each 20-meter transect is shown. Blanks indicate the lack of canopy-height trees (approximately greater than 3 meters tall) within the 10-meter section.

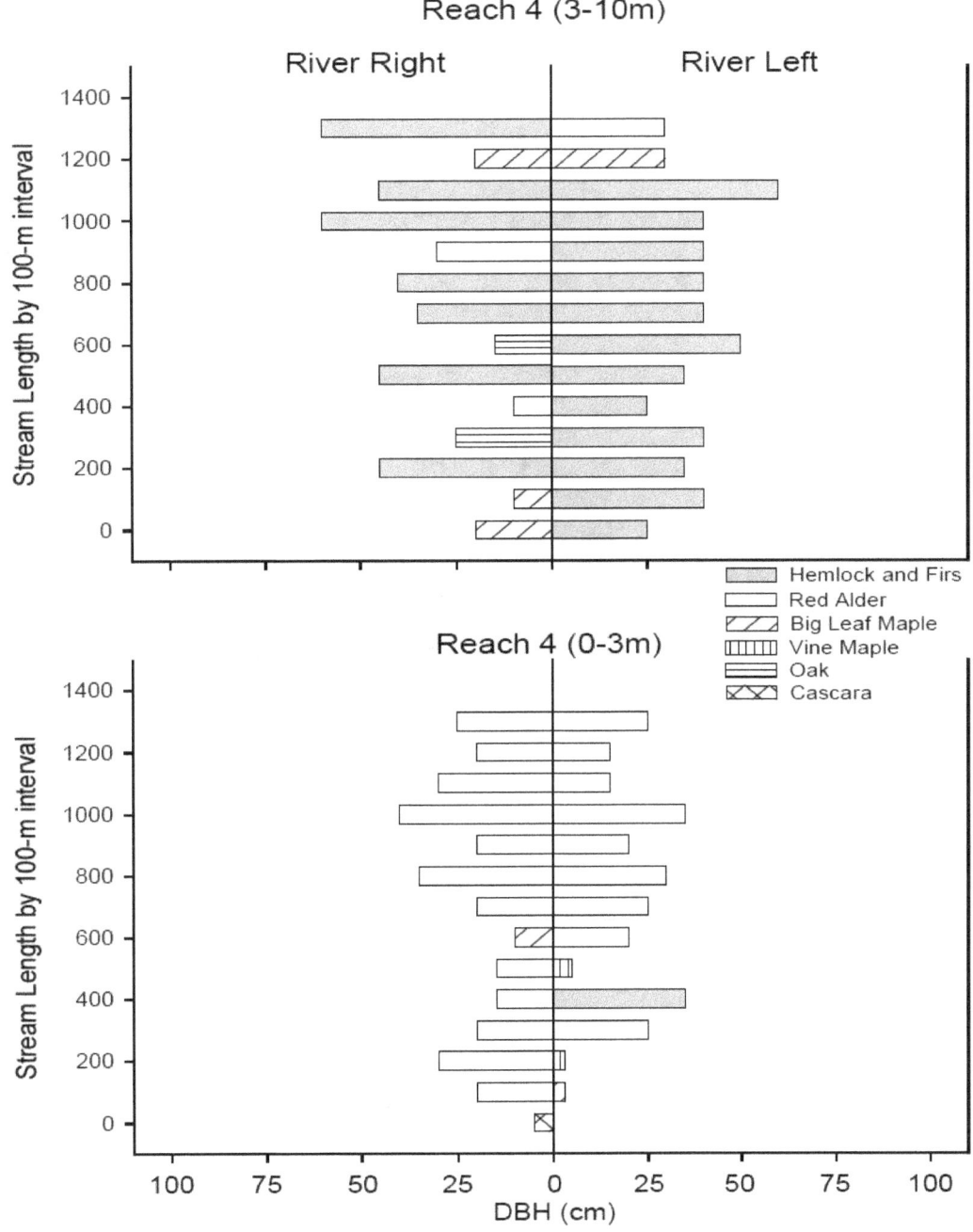

Figure 5. Characterization of outer (3–10 meters from bankfull) and adjacent (0–3 meters from bankfull) riparian vegetation in Reach 4 of Buck Creek, Washington (river kilometers 5.0–6.4). The diameter at breast height (DBH) of the dominant tree type within a 10-meter section at each 20-meter transect is shown. Blanks indicate the lack of canopy-height trees (approximately greater than 3 meters tall) within the 10-meter section.

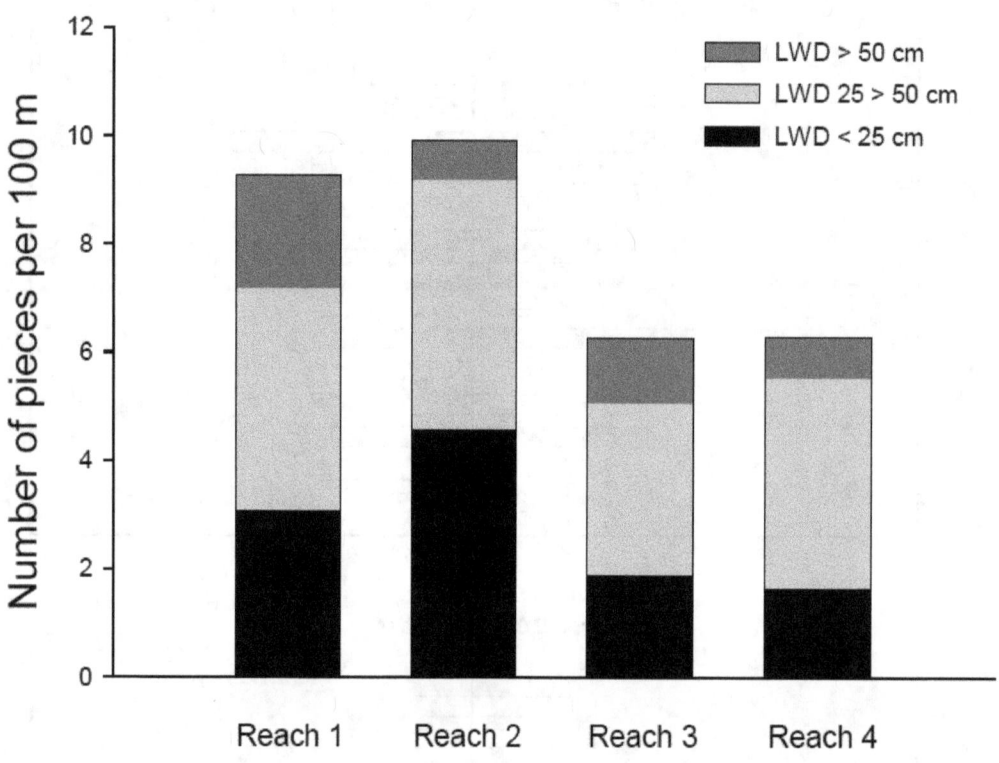

Figure 6. Number of pieces of large woody debris (LWD) per 100 meters in three diameter categories for all four reaches of Buck Creek, Washington. Each piece was at least 10 centimeters in diameter by 2 meters long and within the bankfull width.

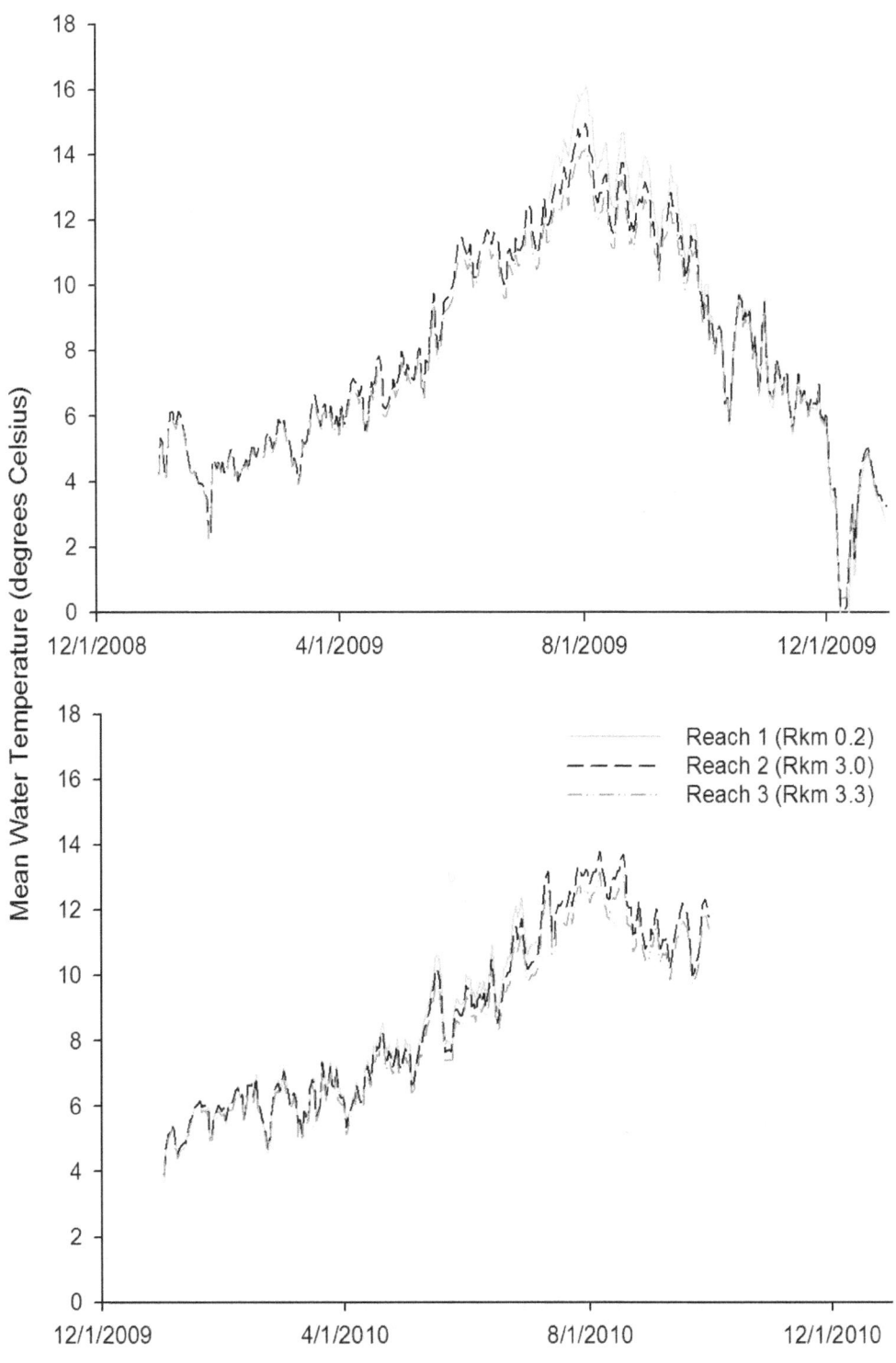

Figure 7. Mean daily water temperature measured at river kilometer 0.2 (Reach 1), river kilometer 3.0 (Reach 2), river kilometer 3.3 (Reach 3) of Buck Creek, Washington. Reach 4 data was not recovered.

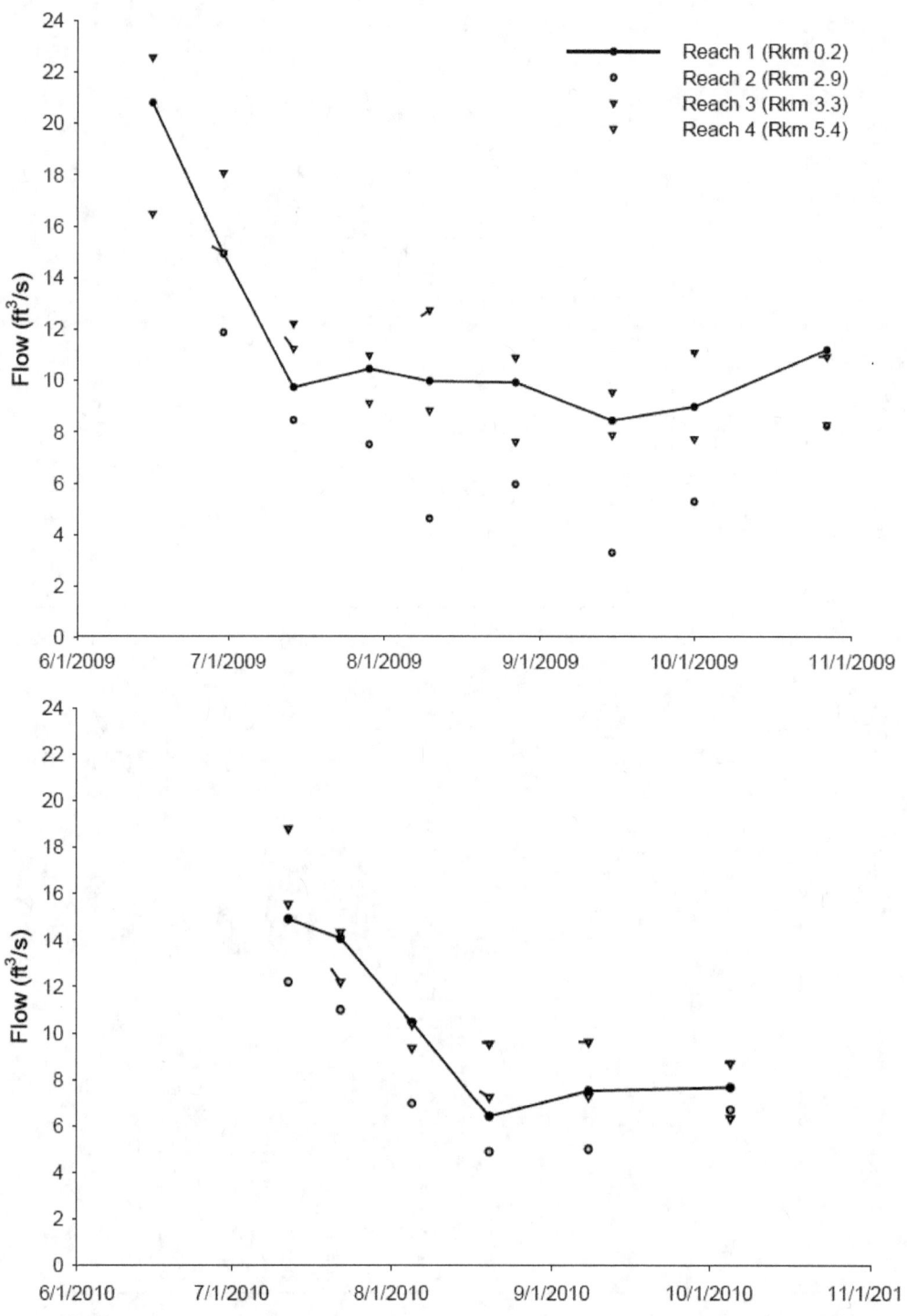

Figure 8. Stream discharge (flow in cubic feet per second [ft³/s] measured every two weeks at river kilometer 0.2 (Reach 1), river kilometer 2.9 (Reach 2), river kilometer 3.3 (Reach 3), and river kilometer 5.4 (Reach 4), Buck Creek, Washington, during the low flow periods, 2009–10.

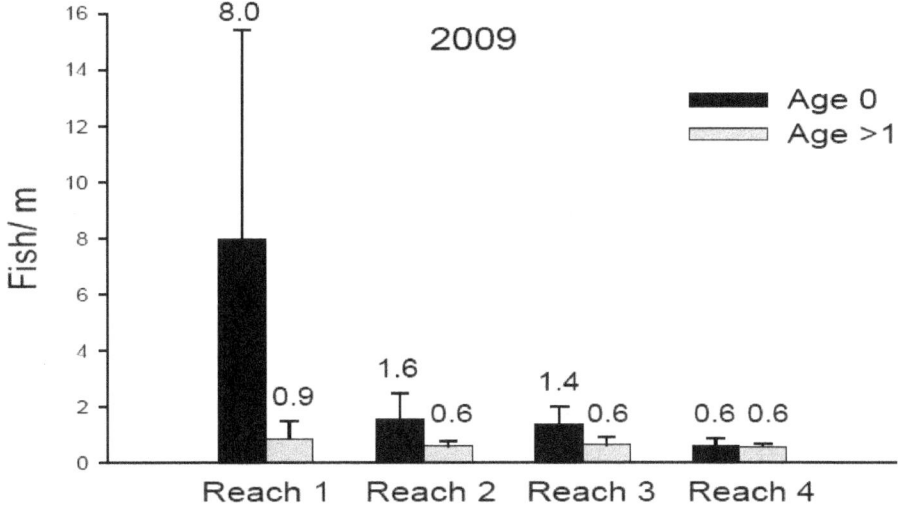

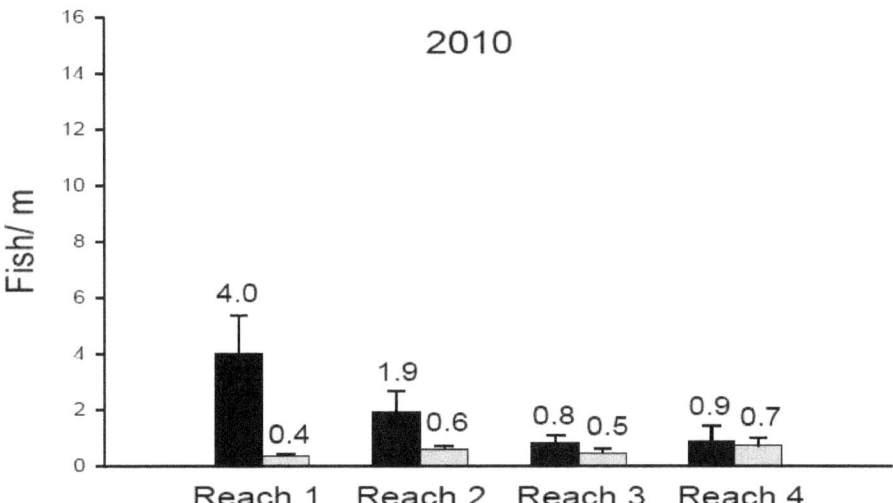

Figure 9. Population estimates of age-0 rainbow trout and age-1 or older rainbow trout in Reaches 1–4 of Buck Creek, Washington, 2009–10. Error bars indicate 95 percent confidence intervals. In Reach 2 in 2009, fish were marked over 2 consecutive days and recaptured on the third day. Fish were marked in a single day on all other occasions.

Figure 10. Average growth per year in length (millimeters) and biomass (grams) of passive integrated responder-tagged rainbow trout in Reaches 1–4 of Buck Creek, Washington. Error bars indicate 95 percent confidence intervals.

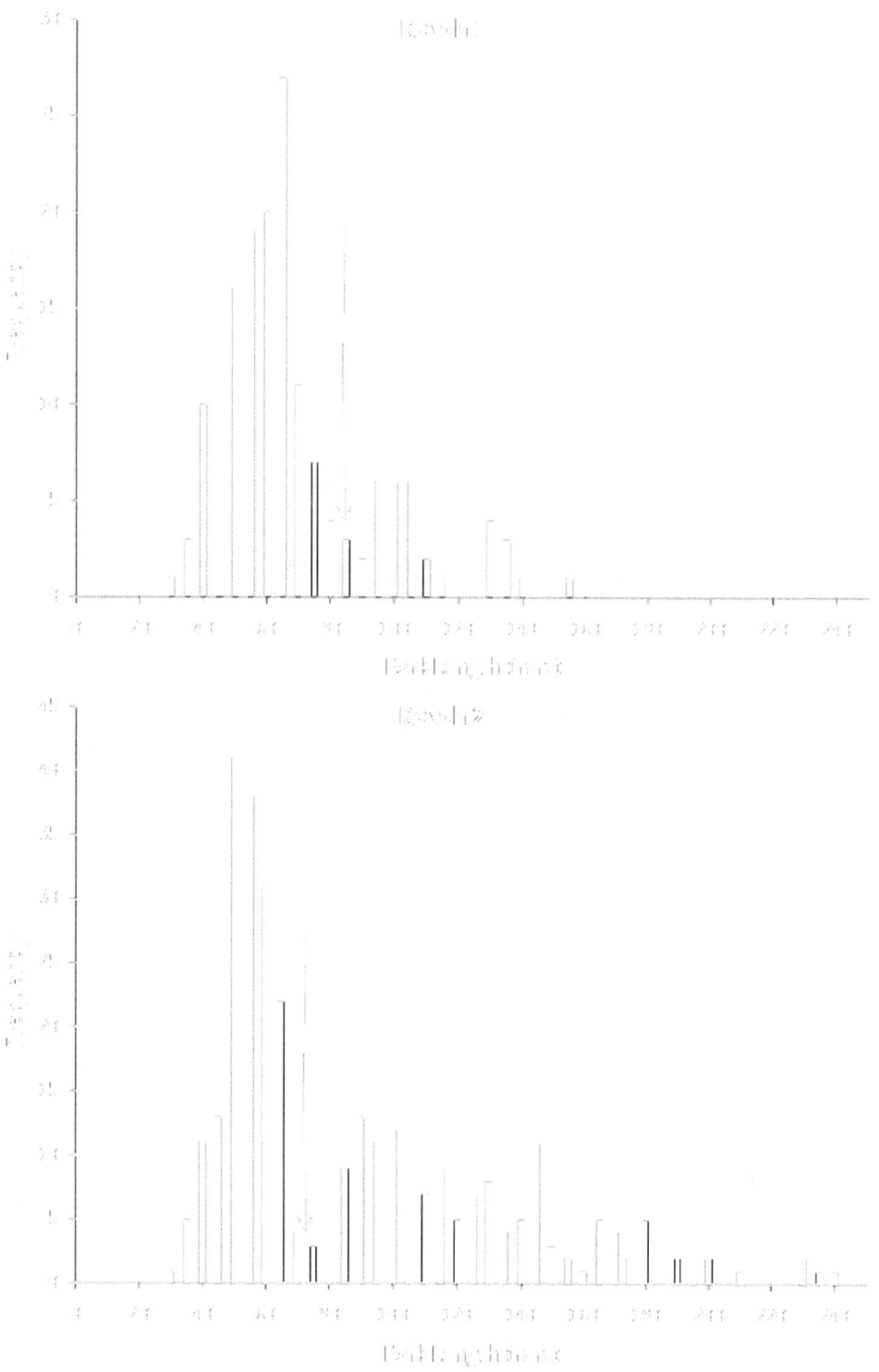

Figure 11. Length frequency in 5-millimeter increments of rainbow trout sampled in Reaches 1 and 2 of Buck Creek, Washington, August 2009. The arrow indicates the break between age-0 fish and age-1 and older fish.

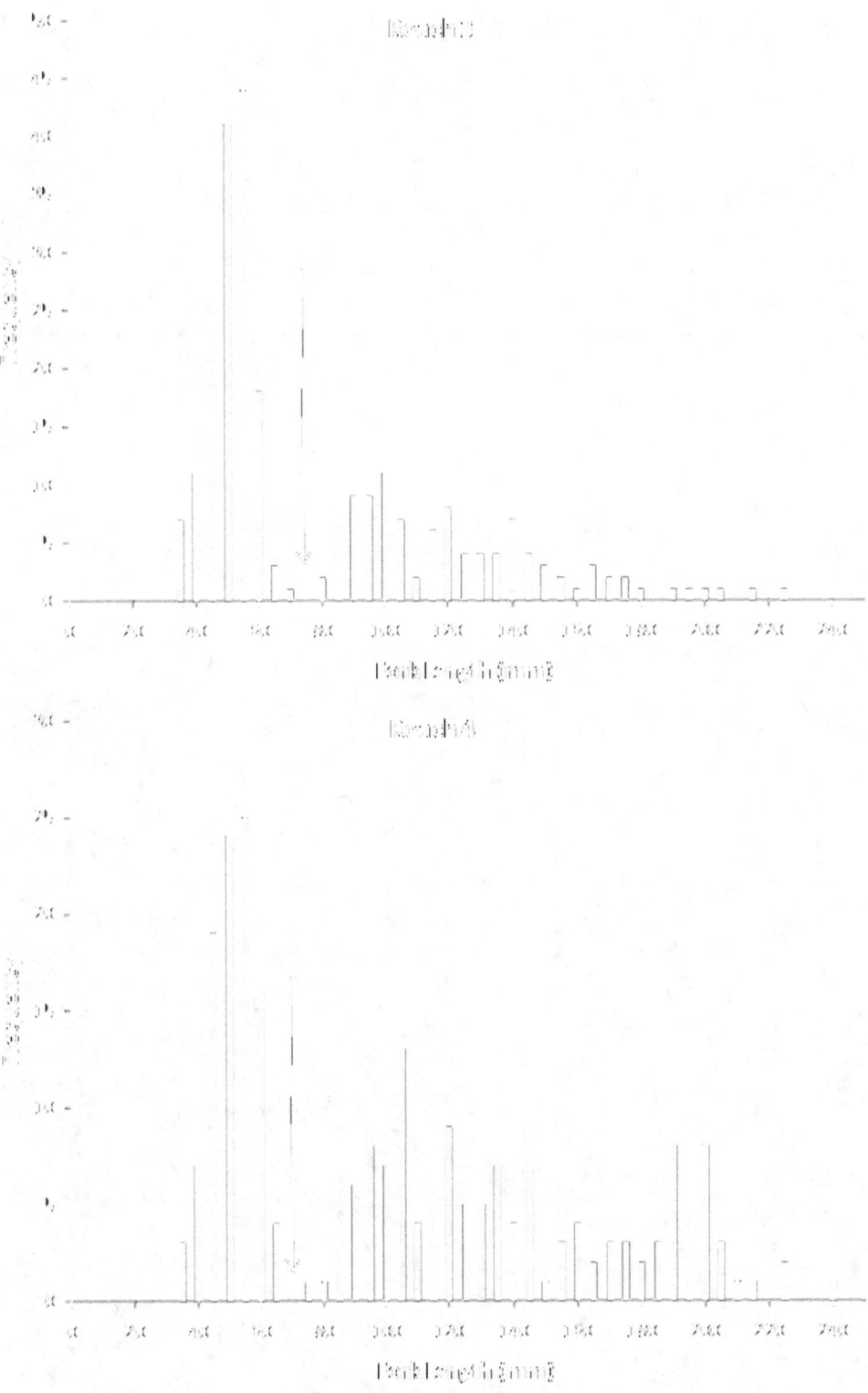

Figure 12. Length frequency in 5-millimeter increments of rainbow trout sampled in Reaches 3 and 4 of Buck Creek, Washington, August 2009. The arrow indicates the break between age-0 fish and age-1 and older fish.

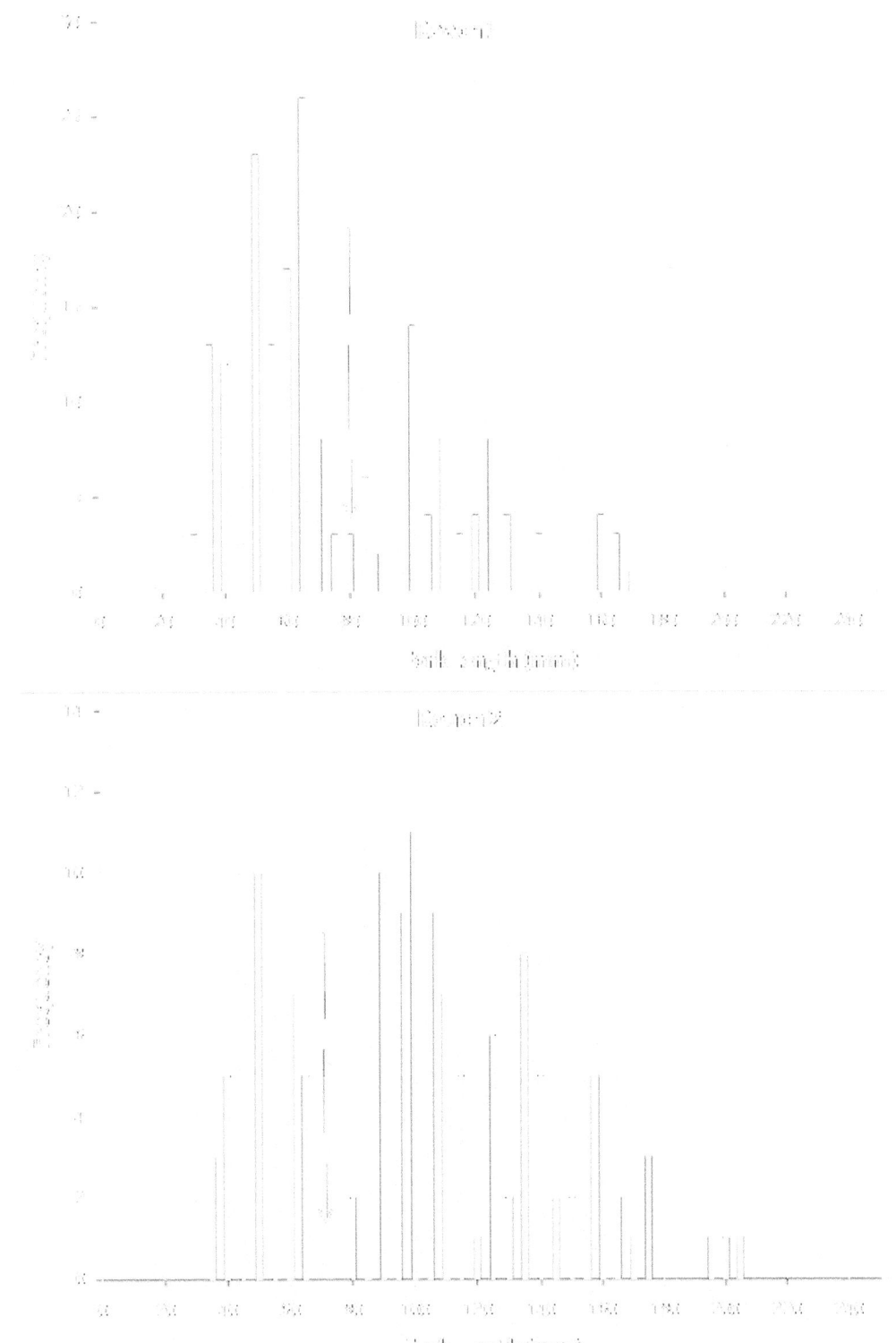

Figure 13. Length frequency in 5-millimeter increments of rainbow trout sampled in Reaches 1 and 2 of Buck Creek, Washington, August 2010. The arrow indicates the break between age-0 fish and age-1 and older fish.

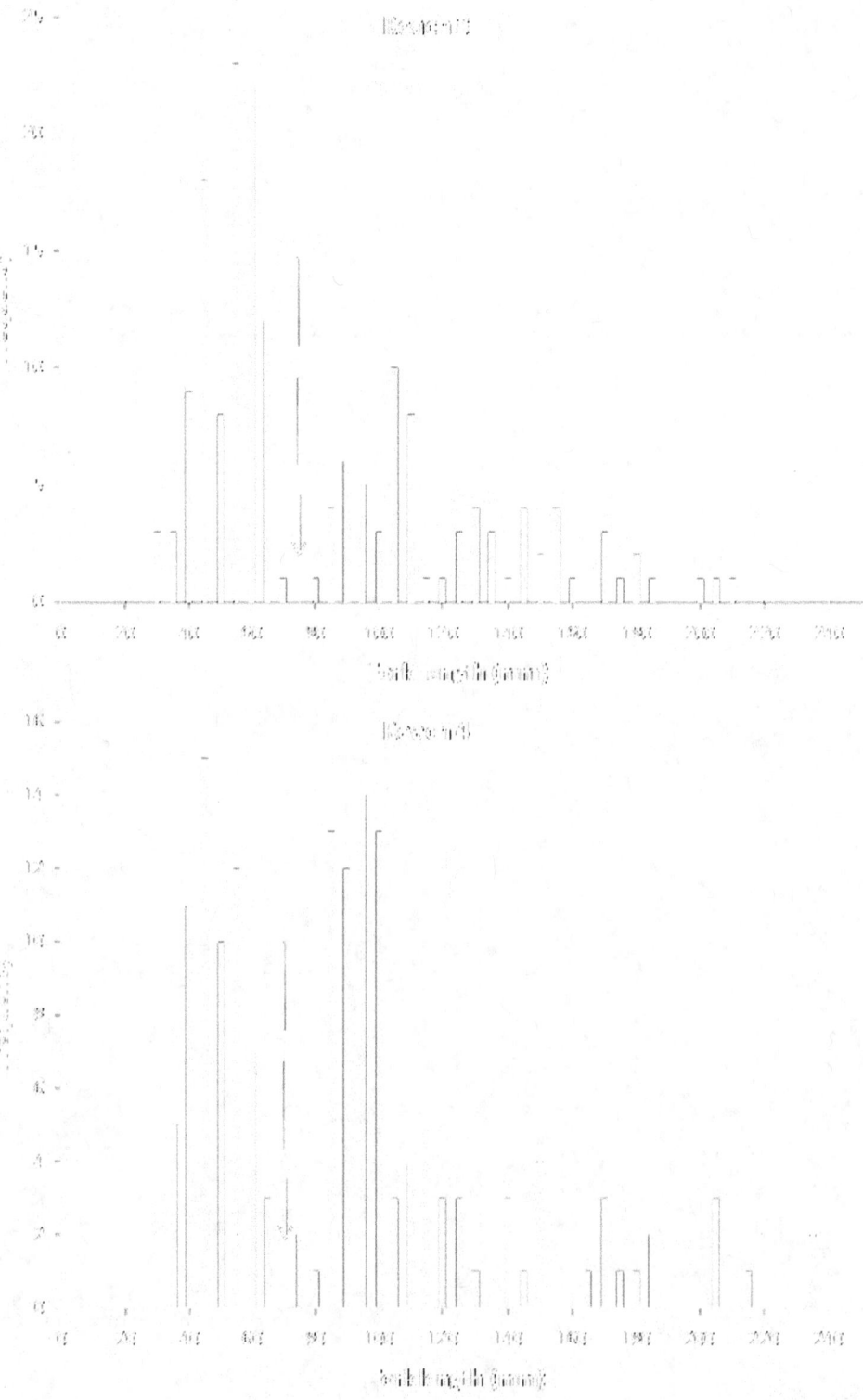

Figure 14. Length frequency in 5-millimeter increments of rainbow trout sampled in Reaches 3 and 4 of Buck Creek, Washington, August 2010. The arrow indicates the break between age-0 fish and age-1 and older fish.

Table 1. Latitude and longitude (decimal degrees) of each reach (start and end), stream discharge site, temperature logger site, and macroinvertebrate sampling site in Buck Creek, Washington, 2009–10.

	Reach			
	1	2	3	4
Reach start				
Latitude	45.78221	45.79520	45.80223	45.81710
Longitude	-121.51723	-121.52880	-121.53457	-121.54316
Reach end				
Latitude	45.78207	45.80209	45.81725	45.82592
Longitude	-121.51676	-121.55345	-121.54300	-121.55181
Stream discharge				
Latitude	45.78202	45.80166	45.80348	45.81955
Longitude	-121.51667	-121.53409	-121.53615	-121.54564
Temperature logger				
Latitude	45.78237	45.79710	45.80389	NA
Longitude	-121.51691	-121.52959	-121.53671	NA
Macroinvertebrate sampling				
Latitude	45.78096	45.79829	45.80422	45.81995
Longitude	-121.51506	-121.53042	-121.53691	-121.54581

Table 2. Survey length, width, confinement, gradient, shade, and habitat types in Buck Creek, 2010.

[Percent habitat type was calculated using area. **Abbreviations:** rkm, river kilometer; m, meter; m^2, square meter; %, percent]

Habitat variable	Reach				
	1	2	3	4	Total
Start of reach (rkm)	0	[1]2.0	3.1	5.0	NA
Total survey length (m)	194	1,088	1,947	1,383	4,612
Total surface area (m^2)	1,419	7,967	11,335	7,645	28,365
Average wetted width (m)	7.4	8.0	6.1	4.9	6.4
Average bankfull width (m)	9.1	9.2	7.2	6.0	7.6
Average terrace width (m)	9.9	10.3	9.4	9.6	9.7
Confinement ratio	1.1	1.1	1.3	1.6	1.3
Gradient (%)	1.1	3.6	4.0	3.6	3.6
Total shade (%)	52	62	58	64	61
Conifer (%)	2	9	4	5	6
Hardwood (%)	44	53	54	60	55
Habitat type (%)					
Glide	15	0	1	2	1
Pool	[2]9	15	14	15	15
Large cobble riffle	54	85	85	83	83
Small cobble riffle	22	0	0	0	1

[1]A distance of 1.8 km between reaches 1 and 2 was not surveyed due to lack of access to private property.
[2]There was only one pool in Reach 1.

Table 3. Number of pools, percent and type of pool cover for fish, percent pool tailout, and mean and maximum pool depth for each reach of Buck Creek, Washington, 2010.

[**Abbreviations:** m, meter; %, percent; cm, centimeter]

Habitat variable	Reach				
	[1]1	2	3	4	Total
Total number of pools	1	15	28	20	64
Pools/ 100 m	0.5	1.4	1.4	1.4	1.4
Total pool cover (%)	55	27	29	28	29
Instream cover (%)					
Large woody debris	0	1.7	1.2	1.0	1.2
Small woody debris	10.0	3.5	2.8	4.0	3.5
Substrate	10.0	14.5	15.1	14.3	14.6
Undercut bank	20.0	2.5	4.8	5.1	4.7
Other	0.0	0.0	2.8	0.2	1.2
Overhead cover (%)					
Large woody debris	0.0	3.7	2.2	1.7	2.4
Small woody debris	15.0	2.3	1.2	2.2	2.1
Other	0.0	0.0	0.0	0.2	0.1
Pool tailout (%)	25	37	30	36	34
Tailout depth (cm)	30	30	36	32	33
Mean pool depth (cm)	85	54	64	74	65
Max pool depth (cm)	100	84	103	105	105

[1]There was only one pool in Reach 1.

Table 4. Average percent substrate type, embeddedness, and fines from each reach of Buck Creek, Washington, 2010.

Habitat variable	Reach				
	1	2	3	4	Total
Substrate Type (%)					
Bedrock	3	3	9	8	6
Boulder	40	91	63	60	64
Large cobble	48	5	21	24	23
Small cobble	5	8	6	4	6
Gravel	0	0	1	0	0
Embeddedness (%)	2.69	1.63	0.04	0.00	0.87
Fines (%)	11	4	3	2	4

Table 5. Number, length, diameter, and function of large woody debris (LWD) in Buck Creek, Washington, 2010.

[To be counted, LWD was at least 10 cm in diameter and 2 m in length. Key LWD was at least 50 cm in diameter at midpoint]

	Reach				
	1	2	3	4	Total
Length of reach (m)	194	1,088	1,947	1,383	4,612
Large woody debris (LWD)					
Total number	19	112	123	91	345
Number of logs	17	103	120	84	324
Number of root wads	1	5	2	3	11
Number of log jams	1	4	1	4	10
Number/100m	10	10	6	7	7
Number of key pieces	1	8	17	18	44
Percent conifer	44	44	52	59	51
Percent deciduous	28	35	29	22	29
Percent unknown	28	21	19	20	20
Mean log size					
Mean Length (m)	6.4	6.8	6.8	5.1	6.2
Mean diameter (cm)	37	28	38	32	33
Mean rootwad size					
Mean Length (m)	3.0	4.8	7.5	5.3	5.2
Mean diameter (cm)	65	145	138	149	137
Percent of 20-m reaches without LWD	13	24	47	41	38
Percent of unstable LWD	39	28	49	35	38
Percent of sediment-storing LWD	5	43	23	9	33
Percent of pool-forming LWD	5	18	11	3	12

Table 6. Number of days per year when maximum water temperature exceeded 14, 16, and 18 degrees Celsius, and yearly maximum water temperature recorded at locations in Buck Creek, Washington.

[Temperatures in Reach 1 obtained from Underwood Conservation District. Temperatures in Reach 2 and 3 obtained from Yakama Nation. **Abbreviations:** ND, no data]

	Reach		
	1	2	3
River Kilometer	0.2	3.0	3.3
Number of days > 14			
2009	46	22	13
2010	ND	17	0
Number of days >16			
2009	11	1	0
2010	ND	0	0
Number of days >18			
2009	0	0	0
2010	ND	0	0
Maximum Temperature			
2009	17.2	16.0	15.2
2010	ND	14.7	13.9

[a]The thermograph in Reach 1 was last downloaded in 4 July 2010 after which it was buried in substrate and unrecoverable.

Table 7. Stream discharge measured every two weeks during the low-flow period in Buck Creek, Washington, 2009–2010.

[**Abbreviations:** ft^3/s, cubic feet per second; rkm, river kilometer]

Date	Stream discharge (ft^3/s)			
	Reach 1 (rkm 0.2)	Reach 2 (rkm 2.9)	Reach 3 (rkm 3.3)	Reach 4 (rkm 5.4)
06-16-2009	20.80	NA	22.57	16.50
06-30-2009	14.93	11.88	18.08	14.96
07-14-2009	8.11	8.46	12.22	11.24
07-29-2009	10.45	7.52	10.98	9.13
08-10-2009	9.97	4.62	13.76	8.84
08-27-2009	9.93	5.96	10.89	7.63
09-15-2009	8.45	3.31	9.55	7.89
10-01-2009	8.99	5.30	11.11	7.74
10-27-2009	11.21	8.26	10.94	8.30
07-12-2010	14.91	12.19	18.81	15.56
07-22-2010	14.08	11.00	14.34	12.19
08-05-2010	10.45	6.97	10.37	9.36
08-20-2010	6.42	4.89	9.54	7.25
09-08-2010	7.53	5.00	9.63	7.29
10-05-2010	7.68	6.70	8.72	6.34

Table 8. Benthic index of biological integrity (B-IBI) metric values and scores for macroinvertebrate collected in each reach of Buck Creek, Washington, August 20, 2009.

[In the Pacific Northwest, a regionally calibrated 10-metric IBI has been developed based on benthic invertebrates (B-IBI; Kleindl, 1995; Fore and others. 1996; Karr 1998). To calculate B-IBI scores, we used the Species-Genus procedure at the Puget Sound Stream Benthos website (*http://pugetsoundstreambenthos.org/default.aspx*) and the attributes from the web site *http://pugetsoundstreambenthos.org/Taxa-Attributes.aspx*]

B-IBI metric	Reach							
	1		2		3		4	
	Value	Score	Value	Score	Value	Score	Value	Score
Total taxa richness	58	5	54	5	57	5	55	5
Ephemeroptera richness	9	5	8	3	9	5	9	5
Plecoptera richness	7	3	8	5	9	5	11	5
Trichoptera richness	11	5	12	5	10	5	12	5
Long-lived taxa	7	5	7	5	7	5	7	5
Intolerant taxa	1	1	3	3	5	5	9	5
Percent tolerant individuals	26	3	28	3	17	5	16	5
Clinger taxa	22	5	23	5	20	3	23	5
Percent predator individuals	9	1	12	3	11	3	12	3
Percent dominance	35	5	48	5	45	5	49	5
B-IBI score	38		42		46		48	
Biological condition	Good		Good		Excellent		Excellent	

Table 9. Revised Ecosystem Diagnosis and Treatment Model ratings for Buck Creek, Washington.

[Revised values are in parentheses and attributes were not included unless new data suggested changes. Ratings and rankings of EDT attributes were based on guidance from Lestelle and others (2004). The EDT reach B1 includes Reach 1 and Reach 2 of this report. The EDT reach B2 and B3 are the same as Reach 3 and Reach 4 of this report, respectively. Conditions prior to European-American settlement are considered historic. Current conditions are those estimated by Allen and Connolly (2005), or those measured in this assessment, in parentheses]

Attribute	EDT reaches					
	B1		B2		B3	
	Historic	Current	Historic	Current	Historic	Current
Channel length (miles)	2 (1.9)	2 (1.9)	1.2	1.2	0.9	0.9
Channel width max (ft)	32.7 (29.9)	32.7 (29.9)	29.7 (23.6)	29.7 (23.6)	29.7 (19.6)	29.7 (19.6)
Channel width min (ft)	21.6 (25)	21.6 (25)	20.3	20.3	20.3 (16)	20.3 (16)
Percent gradient	3.3	3.3	4.1 (4.0)	4.1 (4.0)	3.4 (3.6)	3.4 (3.6)
Confinement	2 (4)	2 (4)	3 (4)	3 (4)	4	4
Percent habitat type						
Pool	40	20 (10)	40	20 (10)	40	20 (10)
Pool tail	8	4	8	4	8	4 (5)
Glide	10	15 (2)	10	15 (1)	10	15 (2)
Small cobble riffle	13	9 (1)	13	9 (0)	13	9 (0)
Large cobble riffle	29	52 (83)	29	52 (85)	29	52 (83)
Withdrawal	0	3	0	0 (1)	0	0 (1)
Woody debris	0	2.7 (2.6)	0	3.7 (3.4)	0	2.8 (3.4)
Embeddedness	0.5	0.8 (0.5)	0.5	0.8 (0.5)	0.5	0.8 (0.5)
Fines	1 (0)	2 (1)	1 (0)	2 (0)	1 (0)	2 (0)
Benthic Community Richness	0	0.6 (1.0)	0	0.6 (0)	0	0.6 (0)

Table 10. Presence and absence of fish species collected while electrofishing in Buck Creek, Washington, 2009–10.

[**Abbreviations:** P, present; A, absent]

Reach	Rainbow Trout	Shorthead sculpin	Eastern brook trout	Brook lamprey	Longnose dace
1	P	P	P	P	P
2	P	P	A	A	A
3	P	P	A	A	A
4	P	P	A	A	A

Table 11. Length of stream sampled, and the number of age-0 rainbow trout and age-1 or older rainbow trout that were marked, captured, and recaptured with population estimate and standard error (SE) for each reach in Buck Creek, Washington, August 2009.

[**Abbreviations:** m, meter; yrs, years; No., number]

Reach	Length sampled (m)	Age (yrs)	No. marked	No. captured	No. recaptured	Population estimate	SE
1	165	0	67	57	2	1,315	626
		≥1	27	19	3	140	52
2[a]	508	0	56	110	7	791	236
		≥1	56	97	18	294	48
3	385	0	80	70	10	523	129
		≥1	62	45	11	242	52
4	345	0	36	62	10	212	47
		≥1	78	57	23	191	24

[a] Because the reach was not completed in one day, rainbow trout were marked over two consecutive days and recaptured the third day.

Table 12. Length of stream sampled, and the number of age-0 rainbow trout and age-1 or older rainbow trout that were marked, captured, and recaptured with population estimate and standard error (SE) for each reach in Buck Creek, Washington, August, 2010.

[**Abbreviations:** m, meter; yrs, years; No., number]

Reach	Length sampled (m)	Age (yrs)	No. marked	No. captured	No. recaptured	Population estimate	SE
1	170	0	151	93	20	680	119
		≥1	38	26	16	62	7
2	190	0	77	74	15	366	70
		≥1	59	51	26	116	11
3	204	0	55	43	14	164	29
		≥1	39	32	13	94	15
4	224	0	36	25	4	192	67
		≥1	60	36	13	161	29